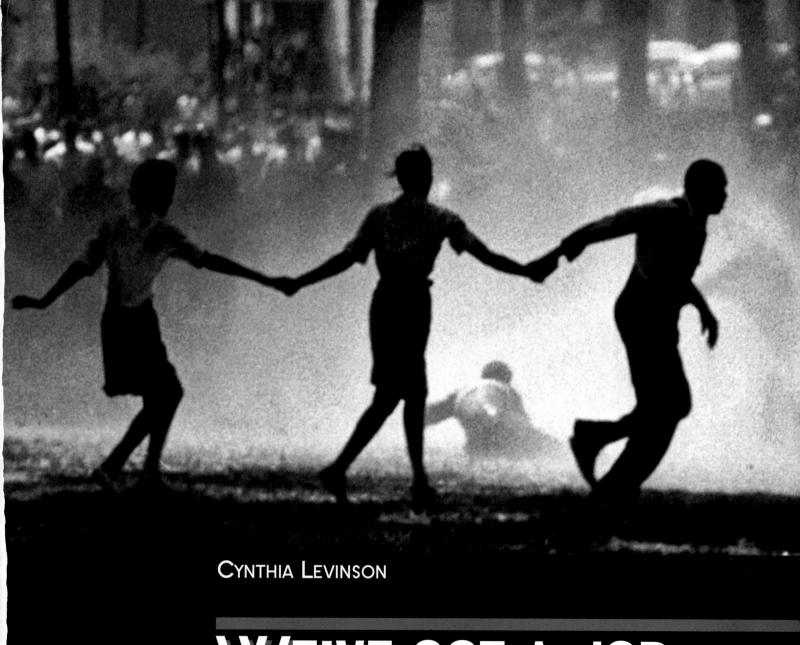

Cynthia Levinson

WE'VE GOT A JOB

THE 1963 BIRMINGHAM CHILDREN'S MARCH

Ω

Published by
PEACHTREE PUBLISHERS
1700 Chattahoochee Avenue
Atlanta, Georgia 30318-2112
www.peachtree-online.com

Book and jacket design by Maureen Withee

Text and titles set in Century Schoolbook
and SF New Republic SC.

Printed in February 2012 by RR Donnelley & Sons
in South China
10 9 8 7 6 5 4 3 2

Library of Congress Cataloging-in-Publication Data

Levinson, Cynthia.
  We've got a job : the 1963 Birmingham Children's March /
written by Cynthia Levinson.
    p. cm.
  ISBN 978-1-56145-627-7 / 1-56145-627-6
  1. African Americans—Civil rights—Alabama—Birmingham—History—20th century—Juvenile literature. 2. Civil
rights movements—Alabama—Birmingham—History—
20th century—Juvenile literature. 3. African American
students—Alabama—Birmingham—History—20th century—Juvenile literature. 4. African American youth—
Alabama—Birmingham—History—20th century—Juvenile
literature. I. Title.

F334.B69N4476 2012
323.1196'0730761781--dc23

To my thoroughly splendid

family—Rachel, Ariel,

Sarah, Meira, Marc,

Rebecca, Gabriella,

and, especially, Sandy,

my *sine qua non*.

And to Peace Ponies

everywhere.

—*C. Y. L.*

CONTENTS

We've got a job,

We've got a job to do.

We can't get freedom

   'til we get through.

PROLOGUE

On Thursday morning, May 2, 1963, nine-year-old Audrey Faye Hendricks woke up with freedom on her mind. But, before she could be free, there was something important she had to do.

"I want to go to jail," Audrey had told her mother.

Since Mr. and Mrs. Hendricks thought that was a good idea, they helped her get ready. Her father had even bought her a new game she'd been eyeing. Audrey imagined that it would entertain her if she got bored during her week on a cell block.

That morning, her mother took her to Center Street Elementary so she could tell her third-grade teacher why she'd be absent. Mrs. Wills cried. Audrey knew she was proud of her.

She also hugged all four grandparents goodbye.

One of her grandmothers assured her, "You'll be fine."

Then Audrey's parents drove her to the church to get arrested.

Wait a minute! What kind of nine-year-old volunteers to go to jail? And what kind of parent would make sure she gets to jail during the first week of May 1963, in Birmingham, Alabama. Their goal was to end segregation in the most racially divided and violent city in America. Many young people suffered attacks by snarling German shepherds and days of being crammed into sweltering jail cells. Some wondered if they would survive. And if they did survive, could they accept these punishments with dignity, as they had been trained to do? Or, would they retaliate against the white policemen who were abusing them?

Audrey and three other young people—Washington Booker III, James Stewart, and Arnetta Streeter—will be your guides through these harrowing events. Along the way, you'll hear from others who lived through these times as well.

A NOTE ON NAME-CALLING

White people in the South sometimes referred to black children as "pickaninnies." This insulting term allowed whites to lump all black children together and ignore them rather than to see each child as an individual.

Whites used even more offensive terms for black adults: "boy," "uncle," "nigra," and "nigger." In return, blacks were expected to call all white people, including children, "Miss" or "Mr." followed by their first name, or else "ma'am" or "sir."

Preferences in how people identify themselves change. In the early twentieth century, black people referred to themselves as "colored" and founded a civil rights organization that they named the National Association for the Advancement of Colored People (NAACP). Today, that term is considered demeaning (although "people of color" is still considered a term of respect). Later, "Negro" was preferred, then "African American." This book uses "black" because that's the term Audrey, Washington, James, and Arnetta use.

CHAPTER ONE

Martin Luther King Jr.
(inset) Audrey Faye Hendricks, age 11

AUDREY FAYE
HENDRICKS

"THERE WASN'T A BOMBING THAT I WASN'T AT."

"NO WAY FOR ME NOT TO BE INVOLVED"

AUDREY LIVED WITH HER PARENTS and her younger sister, Jan, in a tidy brick house that sat on a small plot of trimmed grass in the Titusville (pronounced Tittis-ville) section of southwest Birmingham. Each afternoon, when Audrey came home from Center Street Elementary School, she did her chores, played with other kids in the neighborhood—all of them black, of course—and sat down to dinner with her family.

Audrey's mother, who had graduated from business college, did clerical work for an insurance company owned by a black man. Audrey's father went to elementary school, but starting when he was five, he planted and picked crops with his parents in fields owned by white people around his hometown of Boligee, Alabama. Later, in Birmingham, he worked as a laborer and security guard at a dog food company and at a slaughterhouse.

But the Hendrickses' lives were not as orderly and quiet as this description makes them seem. Audrey was three years old on Christmas night 1956, when the home of a local minister was bombed by a group of segregationists led by Robert "Dynamite Bob" Chambliss. Reverend Fred Shuttlesworth was a good friend of the Hendricks family. Six months earlier, he had founded the Alabama Christian Movement for Human Rights (ACMHR), an organization that urged blacks to demand their rights. In particular, ACMHR had been pressing the city of Birmingham to hire black policemen and to allow blacks to sit beside whites in the front of the bus, in train-station waiting rooms, and even in schools. The explosion literally blew Shuttlesworth into the air and demolished his bedroom and kitchen. Astoundingly, he walked from the rubble uninjured. His wife and their three children were also unharmed.

Audrey knew that this attack against civil rights activists was far from unique. Many black people called their hometown "Bombingham." And, said Audrey, "There wasn't a bombing that I wasn't at."

No one would have blamed Mr. and Mrs. Hendricks if they had decided to keep quiet about civil rights following the bombing of their friend's home. But Audrey's parents weren't intimidated. The very next day, her father and about fifteen other blacks sat down in the front section of a bus, where only whites were permitted. When the driver demanded they move to the back, Audrey's father politely refused, saying "We [are] comfortable where we are sitting." As

a result, Mr. Hendricks was arrested and spent six nights in jail. When he was released, he volunteered to guard the Shuttlesworths' home.

As he drove there one night, more than a dozen police cars, headlights turned off, surrounded him. Told to hand over his driver's license, Mr. Hendricks accidentally pulled his ACMHR membership card from his wallet instead. He heard a policeman ask the others, "What we going to do with this nigger?" After debating whether or not to kill him, the officers decided to let him go. Audrey's father thanked God for saving him that night.

Despite such dangers, ACMHR held mass meetings every Monday night in churches around town. And every Monday night from June 1956 to April 1963, Audrey attended with her family and as many as six hundred other people. Audrey's father sang tenor, alongside three of her uncles and an aunt, in ACMHR's Movement Choir. The choir's director was Carlton Reese, a teenager who wrote the freedom song "We've Got a Job," which he practiced on the upright piano in the Hendricks's living room. It became one of Audrey's favorites.

"It was no way for me not to really be involved," Audrey said. "My parents were involved from the point that I could remember... My church was involved... You were there and just a part of it."

Listening to the grownups talk, she learned the painful details of her hometown's deep-seated racism.

"NEGROES AND WHITE PERSONS NOT TO PLAY TOGETHER"

Segregation in Birmingham wasn't just a way of life. It was the law. The city's Racial Segregation Ordinances, adopted in 1944, demanded almost total separation of blacks and whites.

Many southern cities mandated separate drinking fountains, bathrooms, schools, and seats on buses for blacks and whites. But Birmingham's ordinances went even further: city law and local custom also required separate spelling bees, arts festivals, parties, YWCAs, meeting places, church services, courtroom Bibles for swearing in witnesses, seating in restaurants, and entrances to movie theaters, where, if blacks were allowed to enter at all, they had to sit in the upper balcony.

Blacks worked in white-owned restaurants, but they had to eat their own meals in areas that were separated from both white customers and white employees. The University of Alabama's hospital was segregated by floor, and most white doctors didn't bother to learn the names of black patients, using made-up names, such as "Bo" for all the men and "Bessie" for the women.

SEGREGATION ORDINANCES

Revised periodically, the Ordinances' seven chapters eventuallly covered every aspect of daily life. Here is a small sample.

CHAPTER 14
DRUGS AND FOOD
Sec. 369. Separation of races.

It shall be unlawful to conduct a restaurant or other place for the serving of food in the city, at which white and colored people are served in the same room, unless such white and colored persons are effectively separated by a solid partition extending from the floor upward to a distance of seven feet or higher, and unless a separate entrance from the street is provided for each compartment.

CHAPTER 23
GAMBLING
Sec. 597. Negroes and white persons not to play together.

It shall be unlawful for a negro and a white person to play together or in company with each other in any game of cards or dice, dominoes or checkers. *[In 1950, the City added to the list: baseball, softball, basketball, or similar games.]*

Any person, who, being the owner, proprietor or keeper or superintendent of any tavern, inn, restaurant or other public house or public place, or the clerk, servant or employee of such owner, proprietor, keeper or superintendent, knowingly permits a negro and a white person to play together or in company with each other at any game with cards, dice, dominoes or checkers, or any substitute or device for cards, dice, dominoes or checkers, in his house or on his premises shall, on conviction, be punished as provided in section 4.

During the annual state fair, Thursday night was reserved for "niggers and dogs." Officials even banned a children's book that showed pictures of a white rabbit marrying a black rabbit.

In case blacks somehow forgot who was in charge, chimes in the tower of the Protective Life Building played "Dixie" every noon. This unofficial anthem of the Confederacy reminded listeners that, almost a century after slavery's end, blacks were still not truly free.

SEPARATE BUT EQUAL

Birmingham adopted the Racial Segregation Ordinances during a time when a system called "separate but equal" was legal in America. Developed by the Louisiana Legislature in 1890, this policy was upheld by the U.S. Supreme Court in 1896, in a case called *Plessy v. Ferguson*. The Court wrote that "separate accommodations for the white and colored races" were allowable, as long as the accommodations for each group were equal.

Classroom for African American children in a segregated school

Under this doctrine, Art Hanes, the mayor of Birmingham, could justify segregated parks. "We have four swimming pools for whites and four for Negroes," he pointed out. "Four and four, now how is this discrimination? Have a golf course for 'em. Cost the taxpayers $22,000 a year to subsidize it, for the Negroes to play golf. Now what is so wrong to ask them to play golf on their own golf course...?"

There were several things wrong—above all, the concept of "separate but equal" itself. Separation on the basis of race is simply unjust.

Segregation was a poisonous residue left over from slavery, the Civil War, and Reconstruction, the period when southern whites felt that northerners imposed integration on them against their will. In retaliation, whites established segregation codes and other means to draw strict lines between themselves and blacks.

Not only were the lines unjust, but also the ways of life on either side of those lines were unequal. Public facilities, such as schools, parks, and libraries assigned to blacks, were always inferior to those for whites. And, through laws, customs, and intimidation, whites blocked blacks' access to the better jobs, nicer houses, and greater political influence that whites enjoyed. Black people throughout the South were quarantined and treated as if they might contaminate white people with an infectious disease.

In any case, by 1963, the U.S. Supreme Court, acknowledging these inequities and injustices, had effectively overturned *Plessy*. In a series of decisions beginning in 1954, the Court declared that segregation of public facilities was "inherently unequal" and, therefore, unconstitutional.

Birmingham ignored these decisions. City ordinances continued to enforce segregation of private businesses, which was legal, and of public places, which was not.

"I HAD TO LEARN THE LESSON OF GIVING"

Blacks debated about which tactics to use to end segregation. Audrey's parents tried legal measures. In 1959, they sued the city of Birmingham to integrate its public parks. They won that case, but in 1962, the city closed all of its parks, swimming pools, playgrounds, and golf courses—white as well as black—to avoid having to integrate. The city even filled the holes on the putting greens with concrete.

Other activists used different strategies. Shuttlesworth led protests. One approach was to organize a group of black people who would then defy the law by sitting in the front seats of a bus. Students at Miles, a

local black college, organized bus boycotts, lunch counter and train station sit-ins, and prayer vigils.

In 1962, with help from ACMHR members, the students organized what they called a "Selective Buying Campaign." Birmingham's downtown department stores did not allow blacks to try on clothes before they bought them, eat at their lunch counters, or use their bathrooms. (Some black parents carried a jar with a tight lid in case their children had to go to the bathroom while shopping.) The stores' owners also refused to hire black employees except as janitors.

The Selective Buying Campaign urged black customers not to shop at these stores. The students at Miles hoped that if the businesses lost money as a result, the own-

ers would give in and agree to integrate. Students picketed the stores, carrying signs with messages like, "Don't Shop Where You Can't Eat" and "Wear Your Overalls to Church." They handed black shoppers copies of a poem called "Dollars and Sense," written by C. Herbert Oliver. One verse went like this:

> *I cannot be happy to trade at a place*
> *Where my mother and father have*
>   *suffered disgrace,*
> *Where my children can't work*
>   *because of their race,*
> *Where not one clerk has an ebony face.*

The Hendricks family abided by the campaign and didn't buy new clothes or toys for months. Instead, when Audrey's mother traveled up north to ask white people who supported civil rights to donate money to ACMHR, she also asked them to send toys and clothes for poor black families in Birmingham for Christmas. By mid-December that year, games, puzzles, train sets, dolls, and stuffed animals filled Audrey's living room.

"There was one particular bear," Audrey said. "It was white. I was in love with it."

Her mother told her, "You aren't needy. The people who sent these trusted me to give these things to people who are needy."

Audrey was desolate as she watched her mother wrap the soft, white bear in Christmas paper and ribbons for another child. "I had to give it up. It was tough for me. I had to learn the lesson of giving."

As the daughter of activists, Audrey learned and lived many lessons about racism and witnessed the battles her parents and their friends fought to overcome it.

AUDREY: APRIL 1963

Despite seven years of boycotts, protests, lawsuits, and sit-ins by ACMHR members, Birmingham's blacks remained dismally segregated from the city's whites. Finally, in early 1963, Shuttlesworth called on Dr. Martin Luther King Jr. and Reverend Andrew Young—civil rights leaders with the Southern Christian Leadership Conference (SCLC) in Atlanta, Georgia—for help. King and Young met with local black leaders, including Mrs. Hendricks, to plan new strategies for ending segregation in Birmingham. Sometimes they gathered in Audrey's house, where she got to know these leaders on a nickname basis.

"Mike (that's what we called Martin), Andy, Fred—they'd stand in the kitchen while my mother made dinner," she said. "Mike would lift the top off a pot and say, 'What's cookin', Lola?'"

What they cooked up was a scheme to intensify pressure on the city by increasing both the number of demonstrations and the number of demonstrators. While watching one of these events, Audrey saw an incident that shocked her. "I was standing on the steps of the Sixteenth Street [Baptist] Church, watching an elderly black man walking in the park across the street with other people, two-by-two," she remembered. "A policeman allowed a dog to attack that man—[just] because he was walking. It was unbelievable."

At that moment, nine-year-old Audrey made a decision. She would no longer just attend meetings. Somehow, she would act on her own.

She saw her opportunity before the month was out.

SPECIAL NOTICE!

NEGROES IN BIRMINGHAM and JEFFERSON COUNTY ARE NOW ENGAGED IN A

SELECTIVE BUYING CAMPAIGN!

NOW and as long as segregation remains!

THEY ARE TRADING WITH STORES WHICH RESPECT THEM AS HUMAN BEINGS!

Stop buying where Negroes cannot be hired!!

PLEASE NOTE — AND TELL YOUR FRIENDS:

1.—NEGROES ARE NOT TRADING WITH LOVEMAN'S and PIZITZ STORES!! WHY? — LOVEMAN'S AND PIZITZ REFUSE TO HIRE NEGROES AS CLERKS and SALESMEN ACCORDING TO THE MAY 1963 AGREEMENT!

2.—KRESSES, WOOLWORTH AND BRITTS STORES HAVE NEGROES IN SALESMEN POSITIONS AS AGREED. NEGROES APPRECIATE THIS AND WILL TRADE WITH THESE STORES.

3.—ACHMR Committees are contacting other stores NOW concerning their hiring policies. Watch for other bulletins soon telling what to do.

ATTEND ALL ACMHR MASS MEETINGS—And be ready to ACT as Christian Soldiers for FREEDOM, JUSTICE and HUMAN DIGNITY.

Remember: Our Slogan is: "MORE IN '64"

Alabama Christian Movement For Human Rights, Inc. — Rev. F. L. Shuttlesworth, President
Southern Christian Leadership Conference — Rev. Martin Luther King, Jr., President

A flyer for the Selective Buying Campaign

CHAPTER TWO

Shuttlesworth talks with students in a white waiting room in the Birmingham bus station, 1961
(inset) Washington Booker III as a young teen

WASHINGTON
BOOKER III

"I WAS TOO RAMBUNCTIOUS TO BE A LITTLE BLACK KID IN THE SOUTH. THAT PUT ME IN A POSITION TO BE KILLED."

"WE KNEW THAT THERE WAS SOMETHING BETTER"

WASH BOOKER DIDN'T TAKE A BATH in a tub with hot and cold running water until he was nine years old. He shared one room in a two-story tenement house with his older sister and his mother. The two women slept together in the bed; Wash slept on a rollaway.

Other families lived in the other rooms of the house. Everyone shared a common kitchen and bathroom. The bathroom, which was at the back of the house, scared Wash. "It was little bigger than a closet," he said. "It had a commode that sat right in the middle of the floor. And there was no light."

To take a bath, they first had to lug water to their room from the only sink in the house, near the bathroom. "We had a Number Ten tub," Wash explained, describing the high-sided tin contraption. "We boiled water, poured [it] into the tub, and then put cold water in the tub. And that's what we took a bath in, because there was no such thing as hot water in the house." On cold mornings, "my mom would get up…and make the fire in the coal stove and get back in bed until the room got warm."

13

Toys were scarce. One child in the neighborhood owned a bicycle. Wash and his sister had a wagon. For Christmas one year, they each received a pair of iron roller skates. When those wore out, Wash said, "we would take an old broom and turn it upside down, and that would be our horse. And we would get a coat hanger and make a cowboy gun."

Occasionally, he would get a special treat. "If you were really, really good at church on Sunday," Wash recalled, "and Momma had some extra money, and after you took your church clothes off, and if everything was just right, we would walk down to Ragland's [Drug Store] sometime and get a scoop of hand-packed ice cream. That was the high point of my life."

As a little boy, Wash spotted flashes of other worlds—neighborhoods where middle-class blacks like Audrey lived, and even fancier ones "over the mountain" in Mountain Brook, where his mother worked as a maid for a wealthy white family. "There would be times when we would go riding with somebody we knew that had a car... We would ride through Titusville or over to Mountain Brook... So, we knew that there was something better than the house that we lived in." But anything better than what he had seemed unattainable.

Then, in 1958, when he was nine, his mother got a job as a dental assistant—and a raise. At about the same time, Wash got a job, too. Six days a week for eight years, he woke up by four o'clock in the morning to deliver milk. By the time he got to school each day, he'd already put in almost half a day's work.

With the extra income, the Bookers moved to a housing project. "Loveman's Village was brick," Wash said, "and it was warm and well lit. There was a bathtub. It had hot and cold running water. There was a gas heater with a thermostat that came on whenever it got cold."

Although life was better in the projects than in the tenement house, Wash began to glimpse more of the other world and realize what he was missing. "You'd walk by the Alabama Theatre, and the door would open, and you'd feel that cool air." He also noticed white people eating at the counter at J. J. Newberry's Department Store. "More than anything," he said, "I wanted a banana split behind that counter... But you couldn't go back there." Instead Wash and other blacks had to eat in the basement standing up.

Wash got kicked out of school for the first time when he was in the fourth grade. His teacher threatened to beat him, as teachers commonly did back then, because he was not sitting quietly in his seat. He told her, "You're not whippin' me." She took him to the principal's office. "We went round and round," he said. "I saw an opening, and I shot out the door." The principal didn't allow him to come back to school for a week.

By the time Wash was in seventh grade, he'd skip school for weeks at a time. "My friends and I would go into the woods and build a campfire [or] walk down the railroad tracks," he said. Sometimes he'd go to the colored library, sit in the back room, and read. "It was all an adventure," according to Wash. He liked wearing a Davy Crockett coonskin cap on his adventures.

Wash didn't care if he got in trouble. But his mother did, and she was strict. When they shopped downtown, she insisted that he hold her hand and never touch the merchandise.

"My mother knew that I was too rambunctious to be a little black boy in the South," he said. "That put me in a position to be killed. Sometimes she would beat me. She'd say, 'I'd rather kill you myself than have a white man do it.'"

She was right to worry. There were many white men in Birmingham who might kill him, among them a white policeman named Bull Connor.

Theophilus Eugene Connor was nicknamed "Bull" because he bellowed like one. As commissioner of public safety, Bull Connor oversaw the police and fire departments, public schools, libraries, and the health department in Birmingham. During his second term as commissioner, Connor wrote a letter to President Franklin D. Roosevelt that revealed his views on race: he warned the liberal-leaning president that in cities

15

Bull Connor, 1962

where "the doctrine of white supremacy" fails, "Negroes become impudent, unruly, arrogant, law breaking, violent and insolent." Several years later, a grand jury described Connor as "explosive, vindictive... dictatorial...autocratic and [someone who] uses no persuasion, logic, or reason, if any he has."

Though Connor was commissioner of public safety, blacks knew that it wasn't *their* health and safety he intended to protect. And he certainly didn't put out their fires. Between the late 1940s and early 1960s, more than fifty black homes and churches in Birmingham were bombed. One neighborhood was hit so often, it was called "Dynamite Hill." No one was ever prosecuted, even when the police could identify the bombers.

Wash remembers the police as "the ultimate terror... You saw the police, you ran. It was automatic." Why were the police so frightening? "It was a rare weekend passed," Wash said, "that one or two folk... didn't get killed by the police... This is what they'd do to you: They'd call you and make you stick your head in the window [of the police car]...and then they would roll the window up...all the while calling you 'boy' and 'Nigger'... And then they'd hit you on your head... They'd beat people to death." As a result, he said, parents could scare unruly children into minding them by threatening, "The police gonna get you."

Shuttlesworth estimated that as many as a third of the force were also members of the Ku Klux Klan, a viciously racist organization. A local patrolman admitted, "Everyone thought we were in the Klan," although he claimed he didn't know any Klansmen on the force. "We were just doing what we had to do," he stated.

Almost everyone knew that, card-carrying members or not, the Klan literally got away with murder, with the tacit permission and sometimes encouragement of Connor. And there were lots of Klansmen in town to carry out these despicable crimes: most of the 11,000 members of the KKK in Alabama lived in the Birmingham area.

Connor believed that his responsibility was to enforce the city's laws, and he paid special attention to the Segregation Ordinances, which gave him legal muscle to do whatever he wanted. Since the Ordinances applied equally to both races—they were the only aspect of life in Birmingham that did—blacks were not his only victims; so were whites who pushed for integration.

"YOUR FIFTEEN MINUTES IS UP... THE POLICE ARE COMING"

In 1961, the Congress of Racial Equality (CORE), a group of white and black integrationists, decided to confront bus companies in the Deep South. Earlier U.S. Supreme Court rulings had banned segregated seating on buses that carried passengers across state lines and in the stations' restaurants and waiting rooms, but the bus companies had ignored the ruling for fifteen years. Calling themselves "Freedom Riders," CORE members announced that they were going to ride together "to provoke the southern authorities into arresting us and thereby prod the Justice Department into enforcing the law of the land."

They set out on May 4, 1961, from Washington, DC. Ten days later, in Atlanta, Georgia, they split into two groups; one group rode a Greyhound bus and the other boarded a Trailways. When the Greyhound reached Anniston, Alabama, on the morning of May 14, segregationists were waiting at the station. First, they set the bus on fire, nearly burning the passengers inside alive. Then, as the passengers escaped from the smoke and flames, the segregationists beat them.

Some of the injured Freedom Riders, including several white women, were taken to the hospital but were left untreated and stranded in the hospital basement. Audrey's father, along with a few other Movement members, drove to Anniston—sixty miles

17

from Birmingham—to rescue them. Surrounded by white men pointing guns, they fetched the Freedom Riders from the hospital. Only Mr. Hendricks and one other black man were daring enough to transport the white women back to Birmingham in their cars. There, Audrey's mother gave them food and clean clothes before they returned home.

Connor knew that the Trailways bus was headed to Birmingham. He told local Klansmen that he would give them fifteen minutes to confront the Freedom Riders when they reached town. Then he would send in the police. Birmingham patrolmen were advised, "If a call goes out to go to the bus stations, you don't hear it."

The riot inside the Trailways bus station in Birmingham, 1961

During the fifteen minutes after the bus arrived, racists assaulted not only the Freedom Riders but also other passengers—both black and white—who happened to be on the same bus, as well as bystanders waiting in the station to welcome their friends and family to Birmingham. The assailants also went after local white reporters, destroying cameras, film, and a microphone. Right on schedule, a detective announced, "Your fifteen minutes is up... The police are coming." The attackers slipped away. When Connor was asked why it took so long for his men to drive the four blocks from the police station to the bus station, he explained that they were all at home celebrating Mother's Day.

Only a few of the white assailants were ever prosecuted, and they served only a thirty-day term. The rest of them were never brought to trial or were acquitted. Shuttlesworth, who was leading services at his church at the time of these events, was convicted of breach of peace for inspiring the Freedom Riders to travel to Birmingham and, thus, inciting violence. He was fined $1000 and sentenced to three months at hard labor.

WASH: APRIL 1963

Unlike Audrey, Wash didn't know that black kids were about to offer themselves up for arrest. He passed that spring doing what he'd done for the past six or seven years—hanging out in the woods with friends. He wasn't even going to school very often, much less to mass meetings. When he found out about the marches, he thought the students were crazy.

"It was hard to come to grips with," he said. "We knew [the police] to be torturers, murderers..., and the idea of voluntarily submitting yourself to be taken away with them was just to us—we couldn't..."

CHAPTER THREE

Sit-in at the Birmingham Woolworth's lunch counter
(inset) Chauncey and James Stewart, age 3

JAMES W. STEWART

"EVERYONE LIVED IN THE BLACK COMMUNITY, IF YOU WERE BLACK"

WHEN JAMES STEWART was ten years old, his family's house caught fire. The house was destroyed and his older brother died. To make sure this tragedy never happened to them again, James's parents built a new house of solid brick. There was no other house like it in Titusville. It was built on two lots rather than one, and had a swimming pool in the backyard.

Dr. and Mrs. Stewart could afford such a fine home because they were well-educated professionals. James's mother had earned a master's degree and taught English at Daniel Payne College, a local black school. His father was an internist as well as the first black board-certified obstetrician in Alabama. He delivered most of the black babies in Birmingham and helped found Holy Family Hospital, the only black hospital, located in nearby Ensley. The Stewarts' middle-class status could have set James apart from other kids, but his family made sure that it didn't.

21

Since the city had closed all the pools and parks, lots of kids came to play at James's house and swim in his pool. "Everyone lived in the black community, if you were black," James said. "We were all in there together...and grew up playing with one another." James, in turn, often biked to the housing projects at Loveman's Village where his best friend lived.

Children from the projects were surprised that the Stewarts welcomed them. "They expected," James said, "we would not mix with them." A friend told him, "You and your parents [are] really different...because you let us, from the projects and everywhere else, come...and have fun, just like anybody else." James just thought that's how people were supposed to treat each other.

Like his parents, James was serious about his studies. He skipped a grade at Washington Elementary School, which continued through eighth grade, and entered Ullman High School when he was only twelve. He faced several challenges there, both academic and social. Older, larger guys demanded that other kids pay them "block fees"—payments for safe passage through the hallways. "I really didn't know what a block fee was," James said, "but I learned to pay a few of those in order to survive."

James and several friends decided to meet the academic challenge head-on, too.

"We went to an assembly," he said, "and saw that there were people who were going into the Honor Society with a 3.89, 3.95 [grade-point average], and...a couple of other students and I decided we were going to try to go the first two years and make straight As." James's perseverance paid off; by his junior year, he was earning a 3.9. "The fellows... knew that I could play basketball with them," James said, "but I would go home, clean up, eat dinner, and I would do my homework. I didn't neglect my academics and have Cs and Ds just to be accepted,... and people seemed to accept that."

Ullman's principal, Dr. George Bell, became a model for James. "He was a strong man," James said, "in control of the school. He wanted us to do something with our lives." James admired those traits—strength, control, and dedication to doing something that mattered.

James's academic success also could have set him apart from other kids, but he made a point of being friendly as well as studious. He became active in a social club called the Cavaliers.

James differed from most of his friends and classmates in yet another way: he had lighter skin. His great-grandmother was an enslaved woman who bore a son fathered by her owner. The owner had three white sons as well. When he died, he left instructions to divide his large plantation equally among his four sons. The three white brothers objected; they didn't want a slave's son to get any part of their inheritance. Their father's attorney, however, insisted on honoring the will. So James's family inherited from this man—James's white great-grandfather—180 acres of land. Along with much effort and family teamwork over the generations, this inheritance eventually helped them climb out of poverty and into the middle class.

In addition to property, many of his descendants also inherited a light complexion. "As a lighter-skinned black," James said, "I was called 'high yellow.'" This paler skin tone seemed to carry advantages within the black community in Birmingham. A student said that at Parker High School it seemed "you had to be a certain color" to become a majorette or act in theater productions. Wash believed that some churches wouldn't admit parishioners who didn't pass the "comb test"—having hair you could pull a comb straight through—and the paper-bag test—having skin tone lighter than a grocery sack. Kids repeated and lived by a popular saying: "If you black, get back. If you're brown, stick around." Best of all, "If you white, you all right."

James learned that to "call someone black was a no-no. Those were fighting words." Friends could "make references to my being nearly white…but if I retorted with a comment to someone's skin being darker than mine, then everything stopped… I had reached beyond the limit of what was acceptable." Being called "high yellow" felt like a slap in the face to James, but calling someone "dark" was a downright slur.

"MIDDLE-CLASS BLACKS WERE…VERY CAUTIOUS"

Skin color was not the only perceived division within the black community. No black person liked segregation, but people disagreed about how—or even if—to confront and dismantle it. These splits often cracked along lines of social class. Growing up, James said he learned that "middle-class blacks were…very cautious about their dealing with whites. They had to maintain that balance of pushing without losing everything." Those who had less to lose or who were willing to risk it all tended to be more aggressive.

In May 1954, the U.S. Supreme Court handed down the first in a series of cases outlawing segregation in public schools. Shuttlesworth immediately concluded, "This means that we have the same right everybody else has." He intended to seize that right—and a lot of others.

In his first line of attack, the following year Shuttlesworth drafted a petition calling on the Birmingham police force to hire black patrolmen. His fellow members of the black Baptist Ministers Conference, however, led by J. L. Ware, refused to sign it. Still, Shuttlesworth managed to collect 4,500 signatures from blacks and even 119 from whites. He presented the petition to the city commissioners, but none of them responded.

Shuttlesworth was also active in the local branch of the National Association for the Advancement of Colored People until it was forced to close its doors in May 1956. The all-white University of Alabama had admitted a black woman and then, when officials discovered she was black, refused to enroll her. With the NAACP's help, a black lawyer named Arthur Shores won a lawsuit against the university. When she appeared on campus to register, the white students rioted. The university expelled her "for her own safety" and the state banned the NAACP.

To combat the "helplessness and hopelessness" that seemed to smother black activism, Shuttlesworth spoke out at a meeting at Sardis Baptist Church the week following the ban. "Our citizens are restive under the dismal yoke of segregation…," he told the crowd. "These are the days when men would like to kill hope… But hope is not dead. Hope is alive here tonight." Reverend N. H. Smith Jr. read aloud a proposed Declaration of Principles, which stated, "[W]e express publicly our determination to press persistently for freedom and democracy and the removal from our society any forms of second class citizenship." The thousand or so people in attendance approved the measure with a standing ovation. That evening, the Alabama Christian Movement for Human Rights was founded.

Gathering support for ACMHR from other black ministers in Birmingham, however, was difficult. Most were part of the established middle class, and they quickly opposed Shuttlesworth's new organization. Ware denounced ACMHR as "too militant," forbade other ministers from joining, and organized a rival group to try to end segregation with less combative techniques. Some activists began to call Shuttlesworth "the Wild Man of Birmingham." The president of the local black Baptist seminary actually stated that he supported segregation. Another minister claimed that God told him that Shuttlesworth should cancel the next mass meeting. Shuttlesworth snapped, "Now just when did the Lord start sending my messages through you? You go back and tell the Lord that the meeting is on, and the only way I'll call it off is if He comes down here and tells me Himself." Shuttlesworth didn't cancel, but over the next seven years, only sixty of approximately four hundred black churches in the area—15 percent—ever held mass meetings.

Although Emory Jackson, the prominent editor of the *Birmingham World* newspaper, supported ACMHR, many other influential blacks did not, including Arthur Shores and millionaire insurance executive and motel-owner A. G. Gaston. Hardly any doctors or dentists belonged to the organization, either. Shuttlesworth concluded, "Many of the upper class persons…seem to feel that it is almost taboo to align actively with us."

Many white people considered these upper-class blacks the "responsible Negroes" or "good Negroes." Some had quiet relationships with their white counterparts, which they wanted to preserve, even if that meant that progress was slow.

James learned to figure out which whites could be trusted and which couldn't. "The middle-class blacks had to discern which whites were working together toward progress and which ones were patronizing them," he said. Shuttlesworth trusted hardly any white people; he believed that "a white man smiles like he means 'yes' but he means 'hell no.'"

Across the country, black people argued about the best way to dismantle segregation. Some believed the best route ran through the courthouse. Shuttlesworth had been using this method for years, purposely breaking laws in order to challenge them in court. Others preferred lobbying legislatures to change racist laws, or even running for office themselves. These methods, however, could be unreliable, slow, and expensive. By the early 1960s, activists like Shuttlesworth were ready to take to the streets, holding demonstrations and clashing directly with the police.

"I WAS PETRIFIED, AND I WAS ALONE"

Ultimately, disputes about the best way to integrate hardly mattered in Birmingham. Everyone, black and white, lived under and abided by the Segregation Ordinances.

None of James's advantages protected him from those laws. Despite his light skin color, high family income, and good grades, he still had to sit in the back of the city bus and drink from the colored water fountain like every other black person. Before the Stewarts took car trips, his mother rose at three o'clock in the morning to cook, since they wouldn't be able to eat at restaurants on the road. When he wanted a snack after school, he and his friends had to go to the back of the restaurant across the street; they weren't allowed in the front door.

Odessa Woolfolk was one of James's favorite teachers in the spring of his junior year. She challenged her students to read the newspaper, talk about current events, develop and defend opinions about politics, and apply the civics lessons they studied in class to everyday life. "No one up until that time had asked us what our opinion was," James said. What he learned in her class led him to "look around me and to see some of the things that were incorrect in Birmingham, some of the racism that was actually law at the time, Jim Crow laws."

Odessa Woolfolk in her thirties

One evening he experienced racism first-hand. "I was on the Bessemer Super Highway," he said. "Some boys pulled up behind me very close, and I saw them in my rearview mirror, and this was at night. They were white boys, and they began to yell,...to move very close and flash their lights. So I looked in my rearview mirror. I saw that one or two had hoods on... I was petrified, and I was alone."

The car followed James as he turned onto side streets. He pulled into a stranger's driveway, shut off the headlights, and lay down on the seat. "I heard them turn the corner; they didn't see me pull up, and they went by."

James knew that, no matter what those white boys did to him, Birmingham's strict segregation laws and culture would protect them, not him. He didn't tell his parents about the incident because he didn't want them to keep him inside all the time. "That is the same drive," he realized, "that made me ultimately stand up to the system and say, 'No. I am not going to be confined.'"

JAMES: APRIL 1963

In the spring of 1963, Gertrude Grant, a school friend of James's, started participating in protests. She noticed his growing dismay at Jim Crow laws and talked with him about the civil rights movement. Hoping he would join her, Gertrude took James to watch a sit-in at a segregated lunch counter. He saw white people pour ketchup and crack eggs on the demonstrators' heads.

"There was a growing sense of warfare developing," James said. "Us versus them. They seemed determined to keep us in bondage, which gave us more reasons to resist."

Still, James told Gertrude that sit-ins were not something he could do. He explained to her that he didn't have the fortitude to sit passively under a cascade of garbage; he knew he'd be too tempted to fight back against the egg-throwers, violating the pledge of nonviolence that the protesters had to take.

Instead, he started going to mass meetings. "I began to...listen to the things that the men and women were saying about discrimination and having to make a change," James said. "I felt a sense of resolve. I had enough of the segregation, discrimination, hatred, violence, white signs, colored signs, all of it! Now was the time to confront it all!"

James knew he would have to be strong, take control, and do something to make a change. Sit-ins did not appeal to him. But marching felt right.

CHAPTER FOUR

Training an activist not to respond to abuse, Petersburg Virginia, 1960
(inset) Arnetta Streeter, as a baby

ARNETTA STREETER

"WE NEEDED TO DO SOMETHING RIGHT THEN."

"WE COULD HAVE MADE HISTORY"

WHEN ARNETTA STREETER was in elementary school, she wanted to become a nun. She loved the nuns who taught at St. Mary's, the Catholic school she attended through third grade. Arnetta said they were "very, very strict," and she liked the discipline and high academic expectations.

She and her two younger sisters and their parents were devout churchgoers, attending Mass at Our Lady of Fatima every Sunday. On Saturday, they often went to a different church closer to their home for confession. This church was one of the largest in Birmingham, with mostly white parishioners who always welcomed them.

All of the students at St. Mary's were black, as required by law. But unlike the staff at black public schools, the teachers—all of whom were nuns—were white. So, Arnetta grew up mingling comfortably with white people. In fact, had she wanted to, she could have "passed" for white herself. "Unless you just knew that I was black," she said, "you would not be able to tell."

29

Like James, she was so light-skinned that her friends sometimes called her names. "When they would get angry, they would call me 'half-white'...," she said. "It would really, really hurt my feelings." Although she had friends who passed, "I was black, and it was no doubt about it in my mind," she said. "[I] never had any desires to pass."

Arnetta's father told her and her sisters, "You are made by God." He taught them that their family's light skin didn't make them any better or worse than anyone else. "We...did not think that race should have been an issue," she said.

Mr. Streeter was a barber and owned his own shop. Orphaned as a teenager, he had raised his five younger siblings by cutting hair, stopping only for Army duty and two years of study at Miles College. Mrs. Streeter had graduated from Tuskegee University, just like both of her parents and five of her seven siblings. She worked as the youth director at the black YWCA.

Just before fourth grade, Arnetta asked to switch to public school so she could be with her neighborhood friends. Her parents preferred that she and her sisters stay at St. Mary's but, Arnetta said, "We had a fit." The sisters won the fight, and Arnetta learned she could get what she wanted by making a big fuss.

Washington Elementary, which James and Wash also attended, was a shock to her. All of the teachers were black. The classes were more crowded, and the classrooms were less well equipped than those at St. Mary's.

In addition, she had a long walk to school. Every day, she passed by Elyton Elementary, the white school that was closer to her home. "My father would always say, 'One day, black children will be able to go to Elyton.'" Arnetta wasn't sure she believed that would ever happen.

Her father not only believed that integration was inevitable, he even tried to enlist Arnetta to make it happen. In September 1957, three years after the U.S. Supreme Court ordered racial integration of public schools, ACMHR tried to recruit young people to cross the education color barrier. Several families, including the Shuttlesworths, decided to participate. Arnetta was eleven years old then, and her father wanted her and her sister Joan to integrate a white school, too. The girls panicked. "We were little chickens," Arnetta said. "We cried and thought it was so unfair. We wanted no part of it."

Mr. Streeter wanted to force them to go to the white school, but Mrs. Streeter took the girls' side and he relented. She probably saved them from some pain.

When Reverend and Mrs. Shuttlesworth and their daughters, Pat and Ricky, arrived at Phillips, one of the city's four all-white high schools, a crowd of white men attacked them. They beat and kicked the minister nearly senseless and scarred his face, stabbed Mrs. Shuttlesworth, and slammed the car door on Ricky's ankle.

Not long after that effort failed, Mr. Streeter tried to fight segregation again. The family often went to the movies on Sunday after church. "[M]y daddy decided that we weren't going to sit on the back of the bus that day. He got us and he sat us up in the front...," Arnetta said, "The bus driver pulled over...and he told my father that either he [her father] was going to move back or he [the driver] was going to call the police... We were crying... All we knew was that the bus driver was going to call the police on our daddy."

An older black woman on the bus chastised Arnetta's father, saying, "You don't do anything like that when you have children with you." Once again, Mr. Streeter gave in to his children, to the driver, to the older woman, and to the city's segregation laws. He moved his family to the back of the bus. But he didn't want to; he wanted to change Birmingham instead. Arnetta said, "My daddy often told us that we could have made history 'if y'all wouldn't have cried.'"

Arnetta determined that if she ever had the chance, she would make history. And she would not cry.

After she graduated from Washington Elementary, where she was a drum majorette in the marching band, Arnetta moved on to Ullman High School. In tenth grade, she and seven friends started the Peace Ponies, a social and savings club. Members volunteered to help younger students and saved their money to give to needy families. In early April 1963, the Peace Ponies went to a mass meeting at Sixteenth Street Baptist Church. Martin Luther King Jr. gave the sermon that night.

31

Arnetta Streeter, age 14

"I remember the first time I heard Dr. King speak," Arnetta said. "It was as if he was hypnotizing you... I knew that he was God sent. After we went to that first meeting, we decided that this was something that we were going to do as a project, our club." Inspired by the sermons of King and other ministers and by the glorious singing of the choir, Arnetta and the Peace Ponies got swept up in the fervor of the Movement.

"It was something that was very, very much a part of me. I really, really believed in the Movement," she said. "[W]hen we would leave out of the meeting, it was just like we needed to do something right then."

They soon figured out what they could do. In addition to attending the weekday mass meetings, they would participate in Saturday-morning training sessions where young activists were taught the two fundamental precepts of the civil rights movement. The first of these consisted of using "direct action" strategies to confront injustice, such as picketing stores targeted by the Selective Buying Campaign and holding sit-ins at segregated lunch counters. The other related precept was nonviolence—that is, carrying out these actions quietly and respectfully without resorting to violence, regardless of how white people, including the police, reacted.

King wrote, "To retaliate with hate and bitterness would do nothing but intensify hate in the world... Someone must have sense enough and morality enough to cut off the chain of hate. This can be done only by projecting the ethics of love to the center of our lives."

His message wasn't simply "Love your neighbor." It was also "Love your enemy." He drew this message from the book of Matthew: "Love your enemies; do good to them that hate you. And pray for them that persecute and calumniate you." Richard Boone, an organizer, explained, "You hate the deed. But you never hate the person."

The previous year, before a large crowd in Birmingham, King had demonstrated the true meaning of this credo. As King finished speaking, a young white man named Roy James jumped onto the stage and attacked him with brass knuckles, slugging him in the back and jaw. Rather than return the blows or even cover his face, King dropped his hands by his side and looked at his assailant. Other ministers rushed to restrain James, but King stopped them.

"Don't touch him," he cried. "We have to pray for him." King put his arm around the man who had been attacking him. They talked quietly. The man, a member of the American Nazi Party, started crying and admitted that he had come there to prove that King was not nonviolent. The minister did not even press charges.

For King and his followers, the only moral way to overcome injustice was through direct action that was nonviolent. They also believed that this was the only practical approach. Protesters who engaged in direct action would be breaking the city's Segregation Ordinances and would therefore be subject to arrest. The key was that the protesters could neither resist arrest nor retaliate—no matter what anyone did to them, they were not to fight back. Many people found this lesson difficult to accept, especially if it meant they were expected to love Connor and his aggressively violent police force. Reverend Tony Cooper, a Movement organizer, confessed that nonviolence "was a beautiful concept... But when you're getting your head knocked in, you really gotta think hard."

"THEY TAUGHT US NOT TO BE AFRAID"

Arnetta needed to think hard about whether she was so committed to the Movement that she was willing to risk her safety, and maybe even her life. So she, along with the rest of the Peace Ponies, attended nonviolence workshops.

Lucinda Robey, a friend of Arnetta's mother, recruited interested youngsters to participate in the Movement. She picked Arnetta up and drove her to the training, which was held in the basement of Sixteenth Street Baptist Church. Arnetta discovered that the sessions were as tough as boot camp, and the teachers were as tough as the nuns at St. Mary's. Officially, these teachers were ministers, community leaders, organizers, and other professionals. Technically, they were also criminals—picketers, marchers, freedom riders, and other civil rights protesters who had violated segregation laws throughout the South. For these crimes, they had been harassed, beaten, and jailed—punishments Arnetta knew she might also have to endure. She received detailed instructions about where to march, how long it should take to get there, and what to say and not say to police.

"They prepared us," Arnetta said. "They knew that if we picketed, we would be arrested. They told us distinctly, if they ask you where your mother or father work, you were not to tell them because the repercussions could hurt your parents... We were told to say, 'No comment.'"

The trainers knew from experience that police or firemen might try to disperse the marchers with powerful water hoses. "We practiced how to get down and put our hands over our heads so that the water

10 COMMANDMENTS OF NONVIOLENCE

Arnetta and other trainees were required to sign this pledge.

I hereby pledge myself—my person and body—to the nonviolent movement, therefore I will keep the following ten commandments!

MEDITATE daily on the teachings and life of Jesus.

REMEMBER always that the nonviolent movement in Birmingham seeks justice and reconciliation—not victory.

WALK and TALK in the manner of love, for God is love.

PRAY daily to be used by God in order that all men might be free.

SACRIFICE personal wishes in order that all men might be free.

OBSERVE with both friend and foe the ordinary rules of courtesy.

SEEK to perform regular service for others and for the world.

REFRAIN from the violence of fist, tongue, or heart.

STRIVE to be in good spiritual and bodily health.

FOLLOW the directions of the movement and of the captain on a demonstration.

I sign this pledge, having seriously considered what I do and with the determination and will to persevere.

could not hit our head directly," Arnetta said. "Our arms could be like a shield. [I]f we balled up into balls, then the water would not hurt as much."

She even submitted to simulated assaults. "They told us we would be called names. They talked to us about [segregationists] spitting on us or hitting us." Then the trainers—pretending to be segregationists—yelled names, hit them, and spat at them. In some sessions, students had to stand passively without reacting while others chanted to their faces, "Catch me a nigger by the toe."

To help the teens weigh the risks and ponder if they could remain nonviolent, workshop leaders got them to talk about how they felt. Bernard Lafayette, one of the trainers, said, "We didn't want anyone to... participate in the demonstrations and then regret that they did." He found it was "easier for the girls to talk about feelings than boys... The boys would...fold their arms, look pensive... Not fighting back...the question was, 'was that a manly thing to do?'"

Lafayette explained to the participants that there were different ways to fight. "Nonviolence means fighting back. But you're fighting back with another purpose and other weapons. Your fight is to win the enemy over, not to destroy him." He added, "This was a nonviolent academy, equivalent to West Point. We were warriors." King described them as an army that would "sing but not slay."

At each stage of training, participants had to decide whether or not to accept the risks and whether or not to proceed to the next step. Those who completed the training then had to ask workshop leaders for permission to join the ranks of protesters. Despite the risks, Arnetta and the Peace Ponies resolved to demonstrate. "They taught us not to be afraid," she said.

ARNETTA: APRIL 1963

Arnetta and the Peace Ponies spent several weekends in April in training. The final requirement for the young protesters was to take the pledge to remain nonviolent, no matter what.

"We had to sign a form that you were willing to march, that you were going to be nonviolent," Arnetta said. "It was very, very important for you to understand. If you could not be nonviolent, they could not use you."

Each Peace Pony signed the pledge, committing herself to nonviolence. Everyone knew that the Miles College students who were holding sit-ins at lunch counters had been assaulted, and that those who were picketing stores had been arrested. Nevertheless, after weeks of training, Arnetta said, "We could hardly wait until they started the demonstrations."

CHAPTER FIVE

A mass meeting in Harlem, New York, in the 1940s

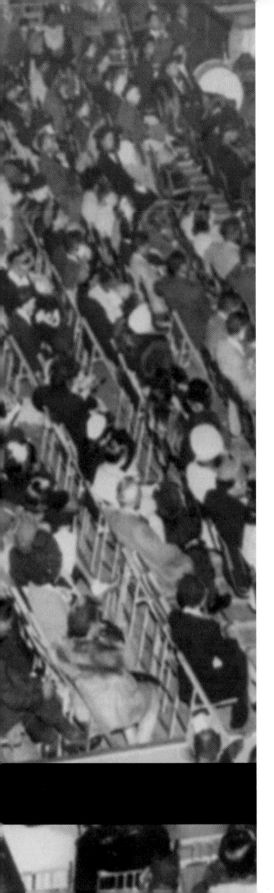

COLLISION COURSE

"NEVER HAVE ANY CLOSE CONTACTS"

AUDREY, WASH, JAMES, AND ARNETTA grew up in their own world. They and everyone they knew were born in one of two segregated places—either in a general hospital in the area designated for blacks only, or in the black hospital, in which case they were delivered by James's father or another black doctor. (The three dozen black physicians in town couldn't practice at the white university hospital, even on the floors where their patients were staying.) In elementary school, they joined black scout troops or participated in activities at the black YWCA, some of which were organized by Arnetta's mother. In high school, they joined black social clubs, like the Cavaliers, the Cavalettes (its sister club), and the Peace Ponies. They were taught by black teachers in public school, sang and prayed at black churches, competed in black bowling clubs, and listened to music played on the radio by black DJs (actually, so did many white kids). They got their hair cut by black barbers like Arnetta's father. Their parents bought insurance from A. G. Gaston. When they died, they were buried in one of the two black cemeteries in town. Their world was whole—yet separated, contained, and suppressed by the white world.

37

"We could go months," Wash said, "and never have any close contacts with whites." Holding a conversation, let alone making friends with someone of another race, was nearly impossible.

A few "responsible Negroes" were occasionally invited to meet privately with a few moderate white businessmen. Through the Birmingham chapter of the Alabama Council on Human Relations, an organization established for this purpose, they talked about re-opening the parks and preventing boycotts by black customers of white businesses. But the meetings didn't lead to any changes.

In public, whites and blacks intersected only when blacks
- shopped in the white downtown
- passed whites on the street (black men sometimes stepped off the sidewalk to allow white women to walk past)
- got arrested
- worked as domestics in white households, as Wash's mother did when he was young.

Intersecting in these ways, however, isn't the same as interacting. Wash's view through Newberry's window was a reflection of the lives of just about everyone in Birmingham, on both sides of the glass. Blacks could look but not touch. And whites rarely bothered to turn around and see.

In March 1963, Movement activists were plotting strategies to seize the rights that blacks had been denied. Most whites paid no attention. At the same time, a small group of white merchants, concerned that segregated stores and police brutality were bad for business, were meeting behind the scenes, orchestrating a change in city government in order to oust Connor. Most blacks knew little about those plans.

While it might seem that both groups were headed in the same direction—ending Connor's iron-fisted rule—their strategies and intended outcomes were completely different. A few white storeowners were talking with each other and with a few blacks about allowing black customers to try on clothes in their dressing rooms. But thousands of blacks were shouting at mass meetings that it was time to integrate. *Everything. Now.*

Black leaders and white leaders were on a collision course with no plans to discuss the rules of the road.

"THE NEGRO CHURCH IS TAKING THE LEAD"

In 1957, the year after Shuttlesworth founded the ACMHR, he spoke to black leaders at a prayer pilgrimage in Washington, DC. He said that, in the struggle for civil rights, "the Negro Church is taking the lead... We have arisen to walk with destiny, and we shall march till victory is won." From its exuberant beginnings, the civil rights movement in Birmingham was rooted in the black church and its teachings—led by ministers and hailed by congregants.

By early April 1963, Audrey and her family had been attending ACMHR meetings—always held in churches—every Monday night for nearly seven years. Then King, who had recently started advising ACMHR leaders on strategies to end segregation, suggested holding these mass meetings every night, rather than just once a week. Nightly meetings would allow ministers to rouse their flocks and rally volunteers to demonstrate. Audrey continued participating for almost sixty-five nights in a row, until the day she was arrested. "I don't ever remember a time we were not in the meeting," she said.

"HAVING A HALLELUJAH TIME"

A mass meeting rolled worship services, social visits, teen hangouts, choir concerts, sing-alongs, fish fries, strategy sessions, political debates, news reports, educational assemblies, fundraisers, crowd-rousers, and calls for volunteers all into one spiritual and spirited extravaganza. Teenage activitst Gwendolyn Sanders said, "A typical mass meeting [was] shouting, singing, having a hallelujah time. Meeting, greeting, loving, caring, and sharing." These magnetic gatherings quickly became a vital feature of the civil rights movement.

Some host churches were tidy, steepled, one-story clapboard structures that would fit comfortably on a village green. Others, stolid and stately stone or brick buildings, covered entire city blocks. In Birmingham, Sixteenth Street Baptist Church was the Movement's unofficial headquarters. It was perfectly situated, across the street from Kelly Ingram Park and right between the black and white sections of town. Several thousand boisterous supporters could squeeze into its semicircular rows of green velvet–covered banquettes, admiring the glowing lightbulb cross on the altar.

"Every mass meeting was packed," James said. "Churches were filled to the brim. There was standing room only. People sat around on the floors." Some nights, so many congregants flocked to these hours-long gatherings that the crowds spontaneously overflowed into three or four other churches. Sometimes, young people would hold their own mass meeting at a separate church, where they led their own services and sang in their own choir. Of course, kids didn't always spend the entire evening sitting obediently in their pews and listening to sermons, even when King was speaking. "Being a teenager," Gwen Cook said, "I would be outside and inside." James agreed. "We saw friends from other sides of town."

The agenda generally followed the order of a Sunday morning devotional service, beginning with a half hour of prayers, spirituals, and hymns, some sung slowly, with long, drawn-out syllables.

After the Movement Choir sang one of Carlton Reese's latest compositions, a minister or two delivered sermons. Then ushers took up the offering. In the same way that worship services ended with an invitation for new believers who had found Christ to walk down the aisle for a blessing, mass meetings ended with an invitation for protesters to walk down the aisle to volunteer.

40

Sixteenth Street Baptist Church, Birmingham

King conducted many mass meetings, and Audrey, Arnetta, and James heard him speak, Arnetta said, "numerous times." Dozens of other visiting ministers were also called upon to speak, including Andrew Young and Ralph Abernathy, as were student leaders and ministers-to-be, like Jesse Jackson.

Their sermons were uplifting and their delivery energetic and energizing. These men intoned, sang, whispered, and shouted, rousing participants to a swaying, hollering frenzy and then calming them to quiet thoughtfulness. As the ministers called out their message, congregants responded loudly with their approval. The sermons were inspiring.

"THERE IS A BOMB"

Mass meetings were inspiring, but they were also risky at times, infiltrated by spies and beset by threats. At Connor's direction, sunglasses-wearing plainclothes policemen recorded speakers' names and took notes on plans for demonstrations. Audrey's parents were unconcerned. "We would tell them sometimes," Mr. Hendricks said, "'We appreciate you all being here, but we don't feel comfortable with you.'"

On one occasion, Shuttlesworth said to the detectives, "You all take this down real good, so Bull Connor will know what our

INSPIRING WORDS

This is an excerpt from a sermon delivered by Reverend Ralph Abernathy in May 1963.

The Negroes of Birmingham, Alabama, are sick and tired of segregation.

[Yes!]

We will stick together… Don't let anybody divide us. Don't let anybody separate us.

[No!]

It won't be long before we march into freedom's land.

[Yes! Applause.]…

I'm on my way… I'm not going to let anybody turn me around.

[Right! Amen!]

I'm not going to let Bull Connor turn me 'round.

[No-o-o. Boo!]

Not going to let the city jails turn me 'round.

[No!]

Because I want to be free.

[Yes!]

Not only do I want to be free but I got news for you: I am go-o-o-ing to be free.

[Yeah! Yeah! Applause. Whistles. Amen!]

Keeping moving, Birmingham.

[Yeah!]

41

plans are tomorrow." Still, he admitted, "To be a meeting church was to invite terror from the police and the Klan."

James was present at a particularly terrifying meeting—one that changed his life. While Jesse Jackson was delivering a talk that night, a man walked up to Jackson and handed him a note. Jackson looked at the note, put it in his pocket, and continued his sermon. Five minutes later he read it out loud. "There is a bomb that is going to go off in this church."

Why didn't Jackson warn the congregation, James wanted to know, and tell everyone to get out before it was too late? "I had my feet turned toward the door," he admitted. But Jackson continued. "'If you only knew how many times people have called at every Movement meeting to say there is a bomb threat because they want us to leave. But tonight we are not going anywhere.'"

James stayed in his pew. "After I realized that the purpose was to make us disband…and stop what we were doing, I said, 'No. We are going…to not be moved.' We did not move that night. We stayed… If there was a bomb that goes off, so be it."

That evening, James's attitude toward mass meetings changed. "We knew that when we were going to meetings, it was much more serious than us just getting together as teenagers and sort of hanging out and listening to different speakers talk to us…. They were telling us it's our responsibility. It is up to us to draw a line in the sand…and do something to address the racial problem."

SHADRACH, MESHACH, AND ABEDNEGO

Like Audrey, Arnetta, and James, Wash attended mass meetings, but he never got serious about them. "We just weren't really into the speeches," he admitted. "[W]e'd sit there ten or fifteen minutes, and then we climbed over the balcony and be back outside. We didn't know anything about no Dr. King."

Still, his mother sent him to Sunday school at Zion Hill Baptist, and the stories he heard had as profound an effect on him as Jackson's courage did on James. One of Wash's favorite Bible stories told the miracle of three boys in a fiery furnace: King Nebuchadnezzar had ruled that everyone must bow down and worship his golden statue. When Shadrach, Meshach, and Abednego refused, the furious king had his servants tie them up and throw them into a blazing furnace. The fire was so hot it consumed Nebuchadnezzar's servants. But the three young men walked in the middle of the fire unharmed because they trusted their God.

"Without knowing it," Wash explained, "they had prepared us to face a mighty enemy without fear. We were always taught that, if God was on your side, He would come and deliver you."

Whether they got it through mass meetings or Sunday school, Audrey, James, Arnetta, and Wash had faith in the knowledge that segregation was wrong and that God would protect them if they fought to destroy it.

A NEW DAY DAWNS?

While Audrey, James, Arnetta, and thousands of other blacks were attending mass meetings, changes in the Birmingham city government were in the works—changes that would throw the city into chaos. These developments had begun almost exactly two years earlier, in May 1961, when the Freedom Riders were attacked at the Trailways Bus Station.

Sidney Smyer Sr., the head of the city's chamber of commerce, was an outspoken segregationist. He had traveled to Japan to seek opportunities for Birmingham businesses. When potential Japanese investors showed him international newspapers containing gruesome photographs of the Freedom Rider attacks, Smyer realized that

Sidney Smyer Sr.

his hometown had to resolve its racial problems.

Back in Birmingham, Smyer met with other white community leaders who supported better race relations, including David Vann, a lawyer. These meetings confirmed what they'd suspected: the commissioners who governed the city would never allow any form of integration, even when wealthy white elites sought it.

Birmingham was run by a board of three commissioners. In addition to Connor, J. T.

Waggoner served as commissioner of public improvements and Art Hanes as mayor. All three men were 100 percent committed to enforcing the Segregation Ordinances.

In January 1962, three months after the board voted to close all the parks rather than integrate them, Smyer and several other civic leaders presented a petition to the commissioners at a large public meeting. Titled "A Plea for Courage and Common Sense" and signed by 1,280 white people, the petition objected to the park closures. The commissioners responded by chewing out these prominent citizens in an hour-long, "bombastic and abusive" lecture. One petitioner grumbled, "I never had such an experience in my life."

That experience convinced Smyer, Vann, and the others that the three men who ruled Birmingham had to be replaced. The commissioners had just been elected in October 1961, for terms that were to run until 1965, but these relatively moderate community leaders didn't want to wait. The best strategy seemed to be to replace the entire form of government with a new one that would be larger and therefore more responsive to Birmingham as a whole. They arranged for a referendum, and in November 1962, voters agreed to establish a nine-member city council and a mayor. The election for these seats was scheduled for March 5, 1963.

Hanes decided not to run for office again. There were three new candidates for the position of mayor: Connor; Albert Boutwell, a lawyer who had served as the state's lieutenant governor and was rumored to be more moderate than Connor; and Thomas King, a liberal. The three split the vote and a runoff election between the top two, Connor and Boutwell, was scheduled for April 2, 1963.

Blacks wouldn't vote for Connor but they couldn't affect the outcome. They made up only one-third of the city's population, and only one eligible black person in ten was registered to vote. Wash's mother took the required test four times before she finally passed; she had to name all sixty-seven counties in the state. Audrey's father told her that some tests asked absurd questions: "How high is height? How far is distant? How many bubbles in a bar of soap?"

Boutwell won the runoff election anyway with 58 percent of the vote. White leaders assumed that the results would persuade civil rights activists to cancel the protests they had planned. Once Boutwell and the city council were in office, surely they would modify the Segregation Ordinances. Then there would be no reason to protest. The *Birmingham News* optimistically proclaimed, "New Day Dawns for Birmingham."

But Connor and the other two commissioners refused to leave office. Their terms didn't end for another two-and-a-half years, they argued, and they intended to serve their remaining time. So, for the next thirty-seven days, Birmingham had two city governments, each of which sued the other for control. Meanwhile, until a court decided who was in charge, the three commissioners convened every Tuesday morning in city hall, as if they were still in power. Then, every afternoon, Boutwell and the city council members met in the same chamber, as if they were in control. The two mayors shared the official mayor's office.

Who was running Birmingham? Was there a power vacuum with nobody at the top? Or, a power overload with too many officials giving orders? If blacks held protests, as they had warned they would, who had the authority to decide how the city should respond? If Connor remained in charge, he'd probably keep arresting them. If Boutwell took over—well, no one knew exactly what he would do.

Somebody had to do something.

MEAT LOAF DINNER 60¢

TUNA FISH SALAD SANDWICH 35

BANANA SPLIT 39¢

COUNTER CLOSED

CHAPTER SIX

Sit-in at a Birmingham lunch counter, 1963

PROJECT C

"OVERWHELMED BY A FEELING OF HOPELESSNESS"

PROJECT CONFRONTATION

ON WEDNESDAY, APRIL 3, 1963, King returned to Birmingham from his home in Atlanta. Just days earlier, his wife had given birth to their fourth child. At a mass meeting at St. James Baptist Church that evening, he declared, "We are embarking on a mission to break down the barrier of segregation in Birmingham." With no intention of calling off the protests, he outlined the steps to accomplish this mission.

Wyatt Tee Walker, executive director of the Southern Christian Leadership Conference, soon named King's plan "Project C." The "C" stood for Confrontation. Black adults and college students would confront white Birmingham again and again. They would order food at segregated lunch counters. They would kneel and pray in segregated parks and on the steps of city hall. They would picket stores that maintained segregated dressing rooms, urging shoppers to take their business elsewhere. Walker intended to plan these actions meticulously, measuring the distance between black churches and city hall and counting lunch-counter stools.

With this information, he could compute the time demonstrators would need to march to their destination, assign the right number of protesters to each lunch counter, and estimate the amounts needed for bail.

Though nonviolent, all of these confrontations were illegal. King reasoned that if enough protesters were arrested, they would fill the jails and overwhelm Connor's ability to enforce segregation laws.

But what would it take to fill the jails? How many protesters would be needed? There were two Birmingham city jails: Southside (also called City Jail) and Ensley, as well as a small holding cell at city hall. Together, they could hold a total of 700 prisoners. The Jefferson County Jail could hold an additional 505. These facilities already housed prisoners who had been charged with other crimes, so a reasonable estimate was that Project C would need to convince about a thousand people to get arrested. Could they do it?

"PEOPLE GET TIRED OF BEING TRAMPLED"

Organized protests had succeeded in other cities, including Montgomery, which was just ninety miles away. Riding the bus home from work on the afternoon of December 1, 1955, Rosa Parks was sitting right behind the "segregator," the board that divided the front (white) section from the back (black) section. But the front was filled, and when another white person boarded, the driver ordered the black people in her row to get up and move farther back, where they'd have to stand. The others moved; Parks didn't. Maintaining her demure and dignified demeanor, she refused to give up her seat. Her arrest and jailing sparked anger in the black community. Parks's boss, E. D. Nixon, who was active in the Montgomery NAACP, suggested a one-day boycott of the bus system.

At a packed church meeting that night, King, only twenty-six years old, declared, "there comes a time when people get tired of being trampled over by the iron feet of oppression... But we come here tonight to be saved from that patience that makes us patient with anything less than freedom and justice." The crowd was galvanized; the boycott stretched into 381 days. Finally, in mid-November 1956, the U.S. Supreme Court ruled that the city's bus segregation law was unconstitutional. On December 20, Montgomery desegregated its buses.

The church gathering at which King had spoken became the first of many hundreds of mass meetings. King became recognized as a national leader of the civil rights movement. Direct action became his primary tool.

This tactic of persistent, nonviolent determination was tried again in Greensboro, North Carolina. On February 1, 1960, four freshmen at the all-black North Carolina A&T College spontaneously sat down at the segregated Woolworth's lunch counter. A black waitress bawled them out for embarrassing their race, but they were otherwise ignored. The next day, 29 more students joined them; the following day, 85; then, 300. As word spread through Movement circles and national media, the sit-ins spread, too, to other cities. When Shuttlesworth observed the nicely dressed young people sitting quietly, unserved, at a lunch counter in High Point, North Carolina, he telephoned SCLC's headquarters. "Tell Martin," he said, "that we must get with this." Sit-ins, he realized, could "shake up the world."

By the end of that month, sit-ins had sprung up in thirty-one cities across eight southern states. When King witnessed one in Durham, North Carolina, he predicted that such peaceful protests were "destined to be one of the glowing epics of our time." Authorities finally lost patience with the demonstrators and started arresting them. King urged, "'Let us not fear going to jail... If the officials threaten to arrest us for standing up for our rights, we must answer by saying that we are willing and prepared to fill up the jails of the South." This phrase,

"fill up the jails," soon became his mantra.

After the A&T students left at the end of the school year, local high schoolers took their places and the sit-ins continued. Finally, six months after the sit-ins began, Woolworth's desegregated its lunch counter in Greensboro and, by fall, did so nationally. Eventually, King believed, even Birmingham would have to agree to integrate.

"STUNNING DEFEAT"

Despite the successes in Montgomery and Greensboro, segregation remained an impenetrable wall in Birmingham and elsewhere across the South. On the day that Montgomery desegregated its buses, Shuttlesworth immediately demanded that Birmingham do the same. Five days later, on Christmas, "Dynamite Bob" Chambliss bombed his house. The day after that, the city's three commissioners rejected Shuttlesworth's demand, and he, Audrey's father, and others were arrested for riding in the front of a bus.

Progress came in repeated baby steps; each hard-fought, hard-won accomplishment in one locale amounted to an isolated incident that failed to spread to other communities. Each achievement of a right—to choose any seat on the bus, to sit down at a counter while eating—had to be fought all

49

over again in the town down the road and in the neighboring state's courts. Integration in one town had no effect in others, yet a single setback could threaten to stamp out the Movement across the entire region.

In November 1961, activists tried direct-action techniques to force Albany, Georgia, to desegregate. On November 22, three weeks after the federal Interstate Commerce Commission barred discrimination in interstate travel, three high schoolers and two college students walked into the whites-only waiting room of the Trailways Bus Station. Laurie Pritchett, chief of police, arrested them, just as the students had planned. They were answering King's call to fill up the jails. Over the next several weeks, more than a thousand more protesters descended on Albany.

Pritchett had done his homework, though. He knew the Constitution wouldn't allow him to bar all the demonstrators who gathered to object to the arrests. But he didn't want a crowd so big that it would draw reporters. So, he allowed some picketers to stand in groups or to kneel and pray on scattered street corners. When his police force made arrests—three hundred on the first day alone—they did so politely. Then, rather than try to jam all the prisoners into Albany's thirty-one cell jailhouse, he farmed them out to different jails in surrounding counties.

King arrived in mid-December and held a mass meeting at which he raised the spirits of the frustrated protesters. "Don't get weary," he preached. "We will wear them down with our capacity to suffer." Arrested the next day, he promised to remain in jail with his supporters through Christmas. Except he didn't. Pritchett offered to desegregate the bus station, so King posted bail after two days, leaving behind hundreds of others who were weary and suffering. As soon as he left town, Pritchett reneged on the offer. The protesters felt betrayed by both the police chief and King.

King returned to Albany in July 1962 for sentencing and chose to be jailed rather than pay a fine. However, Pritchett outfoxed him again by secretly paying his bail. Yet again, King's followers watched him walk free while they remained incarcerated. Although 1,200 people had been arrested, no jail was filled, and the town's whites had made no concessions.

Albany was judged a "stunning defeat" for the civil rights movement. The campaign backfired so badly that SCLC nearly went bankrupt. Many people lost faith in King, and the future of his organization looked bleak. One journalist predicted, "The next town he visits to inspire those who are ready to suffer for their rights he will find people saying, 'Remember Albany... [He'll] lead you into trouble with the white folks and then run off and leave you...'" *Time* magazine headlined the fiasco, "King was The Loser—a failure at nonviolence, rejected by his own people."

Nonviolent direct action went into hibernation until January 1963, when Shuttlesworth asked King to come to Birmingham. It wasn't just Birmingham that was at stake by then. So were King's leadership, his strategies, and—possibly—the Movement as a whole.

"YOU'RE NOT GOING TO GIVE US A PERMIT?"

It was under such pressure that Project C rolled out. This time, organizers had to be absolutely certain that the protesters would be arrested and jailed. So, on April 3, 1963, Mrs. Hendricks and a Baptist minister went to Birmingham City Hall. At the office of the commissioner of public safety, they requested a permit to march.

Connor responded, "I'll march you over to the City Jail, that's where I'll march you."

"You're not going to give us a permit?" she asked.

"No, I am not."

"Thank you," she said and left.

Although Mrs. Hendricks didn't get the permit, she did get what she had really come for—confirmation that, having been denied a permit, marchers would likely be arrested and sent to jail.

POINTS FOR PROGRESS

Organizers also knew it was critical to state explicitly to whites (and blacks) why they were protesting, what they wanted, and what the city would have to do to get them to stop. During the first week of April, ACMHR issued a press release publicizing their Points for Progress, or, as they also called it, their "Manifesto."

The press release began with these words: "The Negro community has made it perfectly clear that they will submit to arrest and jailing to demonstrate that they will no longer endure the laws and custom of segregation, brutal treatment by the police and injustice in the courts..."

Local and national dailies published the Points for Progress. So did the black biweekly newspaper, the *Birmingham World*. But despite the media coverage, few whites paid much attention. Many more blacks paid attention, but few took action.

POINTS FOR PROGRESS

1. Desegregation of all store facilities

   - Lunch Counters
   - Rest Rooms
   - Fitting Rooms

2. Immediate up-grading of employment opportunities available for Negroes, and the beginning of a non-discriminatory hiring policy.

3. Merchants request the City Government to drop all charges against those persons arrested while exercising their Constitutionally guaranteed right to peacefully protest.

4. Merchants request the City Government to establish a Bi-racial Committee to deal with future problems of the community and to develop specific plans for:

   - hiring Negroes to the police force
   - alleviation of obstacles in voter registration
   - school desegregation
   - re-opening all municipal facilities on a desegregated basis
   - desegregation of movies and hotels

"FILL THE JAILS?"

From the beginning of Project C, the numbers of people volunteering to be arrested were discouragingly low. On April 3, Walker telephoned three hundred possible protesters—the same number of people arrested on the first day of protests in Albany. Only sixty-five ACMHR members and local black college students showed up. The volunteers held sit-ins at five department stores and drugstore lunch counters. In response, most of the managers closed the counters and turned off the lights, refusing to serve anyone, white or black. Unsure what else they could do, the demonstrators filtered away. At one location, a white man spat in Reverend Calvin Woods's face. The minister smiled at him. At only one store did the management call for the police. Number arrested: 20.

On April 4, 75 volunteers fanned out. Again, most stores closed their counters. Eight blacks tried to order food at drugstore lunch counters. Number arrested: 4.

On April 5, only 50 demonstrators enlisted. Some of them sat in at two drugstore counters. Number arrested: 10.

On April 6, Shuttlesworth changed tactics from sit-ins, which weren't resulting in enough arrests, to what he called "an orderly walk." Just 35 people joined. They walked two-by-two to a park where they knelt, prayed, and sang "We Shall Overcome." Number arrested for parading without the permit Connor refused to grant them: 29. The *New York Times* headlined articles about these disappointing results: "Integration Drive Slows" and "Mass Demonstrations Fail to Develop."

On April 7, Palm Sunday, the numbers swelled to several hundred marchers. Led by Dr. King's brother, Reverend A. D. King, they walked from church toward downtown. When the police captain ordered them to desist, they knelt and prayed. Police unleashed three German shepherds and the dogs knocked down and bit a teenaged observer. Number arrested: 26, including three ministers—A. D. King, John Porter, and "Fireball" Smith—in their Sunday robes.

On April 8, participation plummeted again. Students dashed in and out of stores holding what the *Birmingham News* called "hit-and-run" sit-ins. Number arrested: 0.

On April 9, sit-ins were conducted at four stores. Al Hibbler, a well-known blind black singer who had come down from New Jersey, attempted to join those in jail by picketing a store in white downtown; police arrested then quickly released him. Number arrested: 3.

On April 10, storeowners closed their lunch counters to prevent sit-ins. Instead, eight Miles College students entered the segregated Birmingham Public Library, sat at desks, and read magazines. Some of the white patrons commented, "It stinks in here" and asked the students, "Why don't you go home?" Meanwhile, other black protesters stood on a corner downtown. Number arrested: 39.

On April 11, members of ACMHR distributed 50,000 leaflets to discourage shopping at white stores. A total of 27 people volunteered to march. Number arrested: 12.

"MASS-ACTION STUNTS"

Hundreds—sometimes thousands—of people were flocking to nightly mass meetings, responding exuberantly to the impassioned preachers who spoke there. Why were so few of them willing to walk down the aisle and volunteer for Project C?

Many people who supported the cause in their hearts hesitated to put their bodies on the line. Fears of police brutality and job loss were real. Some were uncertain that direct action was the best strategy, and others were downright opposed to it.

The black community was still far from united, and the divisions between upper- and lower-class blacks and between moderate

53

John Porter and A. D. King march on Palm Sunday, 1963

and activist ministers were becoming increasingly complicated.

Project C had launched on April 3, the day after the election results were announced. Many blacks, as well as whites, hoped that Mayor Boutwell would be more moderate than Connor and his fellow commissioners. If so, the sit-ins and marches—and resulting jailings—would be unnecessary.

In response to the demonstrations, the *Birmingham World* published an editorial on April 10 stating, "much of this direct action seems to be both wasteful and worthless... A new mayor and city administration have just been elected. It is in the best interest of all concerned for a certain degree of restraint to be shown on the part of all responsible citizens." Activists were stunned and dismayed; previously, Emory Jackson, the *World*'s editor, had staunchly supported Shuttlesworth. But now, fearing a repeat of Albany, he dismissed the nonviolent protests as "mass-action stunts."

Even members of the city's Baptist Ministers Conference urged Dr. King, a fellow Baptist minister, to leave town.

Shuttlesworth and King were frustrated and furious with their fellow clergymen. On the morning of Monday, April 8, King scolded the two hundred black ministers at a conference for "ignoring the social conditions that cause men an earthly hell... I'm tired of preachers riding around in big cars, living in fine homes, but not willing to take their part in the fight." His lecture did not win converts. By the end of the meeting, only Reverend John H. Cross, the minister of Sixteenth Street Baptist Church, was persuaded to join the cause.

Shuttlesworth complained that two powerful forces, one white and one black, were squeezing the civil rights movement to death. On one side were "the Klan and the police and on the other side, those Negroes—middle class preachers...and those that go about their business—who should be with you and who are not." Because blacks couldn't agree on what, if anything, to do, the New York Times predicted "the campaign might be temporarily abandoned."

Desperate to save the Birmingham Movement, King tried to rally swarms of volunteers at a full-house mass meeting that Monday night by asserting, "We are going to fill all the jails in Birmingham." He even promised to collect the funds to pay their bail. The crowd clapped and hollered enthusiastically.

But the numbers told a different story. The next day only three people were arrested. By the tenth day of Project C, fewer than 150 people had been arrested—nowhere near enough to fill the jails. Fearful of reprisals, even those who supported Project C could do little more than shout "amen" at mass meetings.

While the leaders continued to argue, Audrey, Arnetta, James, and hundreds of other kids were increasingly excited by what they heard night after night, unaware that the Movement might be disintegrating around them.

"WHY WE CAN'T WAIT"

A crescendo of public criticism very nearly drowned out organizers' calls for volunteers. In a letter to the Birmingham Post-Herald, a white reader asked, "Can't the local Negroes understand that all they have to do is wait a little longer? Then certain white businessmen, politicians and clergymen... will hand them, on a silver platter, more than could ever be gained by marches, sit-ins, and kneel-ins. And there would be no need for going to jail."

A group of moderate white clergymen wrote in a public statement, "We recognize the natural impatience of people who feel that their hopes are slow in being realized.

But we are convinced that these demonstrations are unwise and untimely."

The federal government took the same position. Attorney General Robert F. Kennedy, President John F. Kennedy's brother, suggested, "Perhaps the timing of these demonstrations could be reconsidered."

Some whites were hinting that they would be willing to accept desegregation. Many prominent local blacks were willing to wait for the new mayor to take office. Why did King, Shuttlesworth, and other Movement leaders insist on acting now—especially in such a confrontational way—rather than waiting for the possibility of a more peaceful resolution?

Shuttlesworth answered that question the day after the election. "We're tired of waiting," he fumed. "We've been waiting 340 years for our rights. We want action. We want it now."

The city government was in limbo. No one knew when the courts might finally decide whether Connor and his two fellow commissioners were in or out of office. Boutwell might never be inaugurated.

Even if he did eventually take office, neither Shuttlesworth nor King trusted Boutwell to meet ACMHR's demands. Shuttlesworth told congregants at a mass meeting, "There isn't a whole lot of difference between Mr. Bull and Mr. Boutwell."

He considered both of them racists; one was just more dignified than the other. Boutwell had called the Civil Rights Act of 1957, a weak bill passed during President Eisenhower's second term, a piece of "monstrous legislation." More recently, he accused King and other activists of being outsiders who had come to town "to stir inter-racial discord."

As a result, King believed, "We will be sadly mistaken if we feel that the election of Mr. Boutwell will bring the millennium to Birmingham." Shuttlesworth added, "Boutwell's not very well. He's 'bout well."

As for white moderates who were urging delay, King replied, "I have almost reached the regrettable conclusion that the Negro's great stumbling block in the stride toward freedom is not the…Ku Klux Klanner, but the white moderate who… feels that he can set the time-table for another man's freedom."

Movement leaders were impatient men willing to confront both fearful blacks and obstinate whites because they knew that, as King stated, "'Wait' has almost always meant 'Never.'" At a mass meeting, he contended, "The time is always right to do right."

Boutwell was sworn in to office but he had no more authority—and less power—than Connor, who continued to run much of the city government in the meantime.

Project C seemed to be failing, and people were losing interest. Attendance at some mass meetings was dropping. Fewer volunteers were walking down church aisles. The national press was turning its attention elsewhere. If it was to survive, Project C badly needed people to sit up and take notice.

On April 10, King announced that he, Shuttlesworth, and Abernathy would march together in two days, on Good Friday. He hoped others would join them. To encourage participation, he promised that the organization would post bond for anyone arrested who needed to return to work and family.

At 1:15 a.m. on April 11, though, Connor served King with an injunction forbidding him, the other leaders, and their organizations "from engaging in, sponsoring, promoting or encouraging mass street parades, marches, picketing, sit-ins, and other actions likely to cause a breach of the peace." To march, King would have to defy the court-ordered injunction—a serious breach of the law. But, if he didn't march, he would have to break the promise he'd just made—a serious breach of trust.

Later on the same day, Connor directed the bail bond company to stop posting bonds for the protesters, claiming that the SCLC didn't have enough money to cover them. This move left King in a no-win predicament: in order to post bail for those who had been arrested (and for those who he hoped would march with him the next day), King needed to head north immediately on a fundraising tour. If he left town, though, he wouldn't be able to march as he had promised. If he stayed and marched, in defiance of the injunction, he would be arrested and unable to raise the promised bail money.

"Good Friday morning, early, I sat in Room 30 of the Gaston Motel," King wrote, "discussing this crisis with twenty-four key people. As we talked, a sense of doom began to pervade the room... Our most dedicated and devoted leaders were overwhelmed by a feeling of hopelessness. No one knew what to say, for no one knew what to do. Finally someone spoke up... 'Martin,' he said, 'this means you can't go to jail. We need money. A lot of money. If you go to jail...the battle of Birmingham is lost.'" His own father, Reverend M. L. King Sr., not only urged him not to march, he implored him to call off all of the marches. If he did, Project C would end only ten days after it had begun.

Nevertheless, King, along with Shuttlesworth and Abernathy, decided to march on Good Friday after all. He explained to ACMHR and SCLC leaders that, "if the injunction had been issued on [the] basis of equal justice for All, we should abide by it. But our action is based on a Moral Mandate, backed up by a Constitutional Mandate."

Dressed in blue jeans to honor the Selective Buying Campaign, they led fifty activists singing freedom songs along a route lined with nearly a thousand black spectators. Some knelt as the marchers passed. When Connor ordered, "Stop them," two patrolmen blocked their path, and the marchers knelt in prayer. They were arrested, and King and Abernathy spent

Fred Shuttlesworth, Ralph Abernathy, and Martin Luther King Jr. march on Good Friday, 1963

eight days in solitary confinement. During that time, King wrote the now-famous "Letter from Birmingham Jail." Except for a reading on a radio station in New York City, the letter was not made public until the following summer.

On April 12, dozens of people defied an injunction against marching. Number arrested: 46, including three very prominent preachers.

"BIRMINGHAM IS SICK!"

With King, Shuttlesworth, and Abernathy in jail, a new minister spoke at the mass meeting on the evening of April 12, Good Friday. A former pop musician with a recording contract, twenty-six-year-old James Bevel captured the attention of the young people. He sometimes described himself as a "chicken-eating, liquor-drinking, woman-chasing Baptist preacher." He topped his shaved head with a skullcap and wore blue-jean suits covered in buttons. James said, "He had SNCC, CORE, SCLC, all the movements. He looked like he was not too much older than us."

"Birmingham is sick," Bevel called down from the pulpit of Sixteenth Street Baptist Church. Both blacks and whites "are so sick that they can't see what segregation has done to them." He turned directly to the policemen recording the meeting and said,

"You can put me in jail but you can't stop us." Then, to the congregants, he added, "The Negro has been sitting here dead for three hundred years. It is time he got up and walked."

With that, James said, Bevel "became the pied piper for the young people."

Only a few hundred adults heard Bevel's frenzied sermon that night, and just seventeen volunteered to go to jail. But kids got the message, especially when the preacher who followed Bevel proclaimed, "Some of these students say they have got to go to school, but they will get more education in five days in the City Jail than they will get in five months in a segregated school."

While Movement leaders despaired because grown-ups refused to walk down the aisle and continued shopping in segregated stores, young people began to heed the call. Finally, someone was talking their language.

Arnetta and the Peace Ponies pulled out their walking shoes.

CHAPTER SEVEN

James Bevel and Martin Luther King Jr., 1965

THE FOOT SOLDIERS

"WE GOT TO USE WHAT WE GOT."

JAMES BEVEL INTENDED FOR HIS language to upset people, especially kids. At Saturday morning nonviolence training sessions, he harangued the young participants.

"[Y]ou are responsible for segregation," Bevel proclaimed, "you and your parents because you have not stood up… [N]o one has the power to oppress you if you don't cooperate. So, if you say you are oppressed, then you are…in league with the oppressor; now, it's your responsibility to break the league with him."

Arnetta and her friends found Bevel inspiring. Other kids were insulted and some shamed by the charge that they were aiding the enemy. Why would a minister blame young people for conditions that were beyond their control—that had been beyond every black person's control for well over a century?

The leadership of the civil rights movement was growing desperate. The future of the Movement seemed to hinge on what happened in Birmingham. But Project C wasn't attracting nearly enough volunteers. Fewer than 150 demonstrators had been jailed. Dr. King was incommunicado, in solitary confinement, following his Good Friday arrest. The national press was abandoning Birmingham.

61

So Bevel turned to young people. "A boy in high school, he can get the same effect in terms of being in jail...as his father," he reasoned, "yet, there is no economic threat on the family because the father is still on the job."

The argument made sense economically, but it was a dangerous strategy, not only for the "boy in high school" but also for girls who, it turned out, became the first responders.

"I WAS ARRESTED FOR THE FIRST TIME"

On the Sunday after Bevel materialized at Sixteenth Street Baptist Church, Arnetta plunged into her first demonstration. She met up with a group that included the other Peace Ponies, twelve to fifteen Miles College students, and several preachers. They walked from downtown to city hall, knelt on the steps, prayed, and sang. They were not arrested.

62

Protest outside a lunch counter, Birmingham

"The next Saturday," she said, "I was arrested for the first time." That morning, April 20, Arnetta put on new clothes and told her parents she was going bowling with the Peace Ponies. Instead, Mrs. Robey again drove her downtown. "I lied to my parents about where I was going," Arnetta said. "I didn't have my parents' permission to go to jail."

Arnetta didn't want her mother to worry when she failed to come home, so Mrs. Robey promised that she would tell Mrs. Streeter where her daughter had gone. She dropped Arnetta off at the intersection of Third Avenue North and Nineteenth Street by Loveman's Department Store. It was next door to J. J. Newberry's where, more than anything, Wash wanted to sit at the counter and eat a banana split.

College students had been picketing both stores. Like every other strategy Project C planners had tried, however, this campaign was failing; black customers continued to spend money at both businesses. Bevel hoped they'd be too embarrassed to shop there if high schoolers picketed.

Holding a sign that read "Freedom Today, Tomorrow," Arnetta walked with six other Peace Ponies from the corner, past Loveman's, to the alley between the two stores. At the alley, police stopped them. Ten minutes into her nonviolent protest, Arnetta was on her way to jail.

When Arnetta heard the doors of the Jefferson County Jail slam behind her, she wondered if her parents were right: maybe she was too young to demonstrate.

"We were fingerprinted," she said. "They took our pictures; then they began to question us." Gaping at her light complexion and long pigtails, a matron asked, "What are *you* doing in here?"

"I want my freedom," Arnetta replied. The matron burst out laughing. "She thought I was not black," Arnetta said. "She felt I was being smart-mouthed." In retaliation, the matron locked Arnetta "in a day room that had no facilities for sleeping... It just had a big iron table. We didn't even have anywhere to sit... The food—there was no way to eat the food. They had us scrubbing, gave us rags to scrub along the front of the cells. If you were too loud... you were given extra duties."

She had no way to know how long she'd be in jail. When she was afraid, she sang freedom songs. "We sang them whenever we had the chance," she said, "and calmed down." About one o'clock Monday morning, on April 22, Arnetta heard someone call her name. A civil rights organizer had put up his house as collateral and bailed her and the other Peace Ponies out of jail. He drove her home. "I had a new sweater," she said. "I ran off and left that sweater. Never looked back."

April 13. Picketers, including students from Ohio and ministers from Connecticut, walked in front of a downtown department store. Number arrested: 6

April 14. Ministers led marchers, supported by over a thousand singing spectators, toward the jail to pray for King and Abernathy. Number arrested: 32

April 15. Sit-ins and pickets were held at two department stores. Number arrested: 9

April 16. Protesters demonstrated at a variety store and a bakery. Number arrested: 7

April 17. A group of 15 women walked toward the courthouse to register to vote but were stopped en route. Number arrested: 7

April 18. Sit-ins were held at two lunch counters. Number arrested: 7, all teenagers

April 19. Sit-ins were held at a lunch counter. Number arrested: 11

Her parents and sisters were awake, waiting for her when she got home. They talked for hours about the demonstrations, nonviolence training, and her involvement. Arnetta's sister Joan decided she wanted to march, too, but Mr. and Mrs. Streeter refused to allow it.

"What am I going to tell my children when they ask me what was I doing during the demonstration?" Joan asked.

Their mother answered, "You tell your children that you were at home crying because you wanted to participate but you were being obedient to your parents, and your sister was being hardheaded."

Mr. and Mrs. Streeter supported integration but were concerned for their daughters' safety. "You've done your part," they told Arnetta. "You need to leave this alone." She convinced them on one issue, though. From then on, they would attend mass meetings with her.

MASS RALLIES. LOW TALLIES

On Tuesday, April 23, Arnetta attended a boisterous mass meeting along with about 1,500 other young blacks and three white college students. The gathering celebrated Dr. King's release from jail and honored the students, like the Peace Ponies, who had been participating in nonviolence workshops.

The students who had demonstrated stood up and testified about their actions. Some described sit-ins at lunch counters where bystanders smeared food on them. Arnetta spoke about her experiences in jail and her regret about losing her sweater. "They were all cheering us on," she said. "They were very proud of us."

Praising the young people, Shuttlesworth shouted, "Keep on walking, keep on sitting-in, keep on picketing." Then, he introduced three white students who were active in the movement. Barbara Jo McBride and Samuel Curtis Shirah Jr. had joined a Miles College march against injustice. Minnie Martha Turnipseed had participated in a sit-in with black students at Woolworth's. Thanking them for their commitment, Shuttlesworth enthusiastically put his arms around the women's shoulders. The crowd cheered again.

Connor's spies were disgusted. A black man touched young white women! The next day, Connor called the dean at Turnipseed's college and she was expelled.

The young people who attended this meeting might have believed that the Movement was successful, that thousands were protesting, that integration was around the corner. Many adults knew better. At other mass meetings that night, congregants learned what happened that day to a white mailman on a one-man Freedom Walk.

PROJECT C SINKS

April 20. Dr. King was released from jail. Demonstrators picketed and held sit-ins at four stores. Number arrested: 15, including Arnetta and the Peace Ponies

April 21. Small groups of worshippers attempted to enter white churches; some were admitted. Number arrested: 0

April 22. Sit-ins were held at three stores. Number arrested: 0

April 23. Five students picketed a downtown store. Number arrested: 5

April 24. Sporadic demonstrations held. Number arrested: 6

April 25. Number arrested: 5

April 26. Number arrested: 4

April 27. Number arrested: 9

April 28. Number arrested: 0

April 29. Number arrested: 0

William Moore had hoped to make the case for racial tolerance by wearing signboards, including "End Segregation in America," while he walked from Chattanooga, Tennessee, to Jackson, Mississippi, where he planned to confront Governor Ross Barnett. Moore was murdered forty miles from Birmingham. No wonder hardly anyone was demonstrating. No matter how long or passionately King exhorted the crowds to volunteer, he could not persuade them to risk their lives. The jails were still nowhere near full, and in the coming days, the prison population barely budged.

Wyatt Tee Walker recognized that the Movement had "run out of troops. We had scraped the bottom of the barrel of adults who could go [to jail]."

On April 29, King called an emergency meeting. Project C was about to collapse. Without hordes of volunteers to flood the jails and attract the press, the campaign to desegregate Birmingham would evaporate. Worse, civil rights victories elsewhere in the country were practically ancient history. It had been more than two years since the Greensboro sit-ins and over six years since the bus boycott in Montgomery. It seemed that the entire Movement was doomed. If King's strategy to fill Birmingham's jails failed, blacks throughout the South could expect to drink from separate water fountains, go to separate schools where they'd use textbooks discarded by white students, take and fail voter registration tests, and get beaten up by policemen and racist thugs for—well, no one knew how long.

The leaders despaired. What should they do?

Bevel answered: Fill the jails with school children.

"RAISE THEM SO THEY'LL BE PEOPLE ON THEIR OWN"

Project C was supposed to pit black activists against white segregationists. Instead, black leaders were confronting each other. Birmingham's black population was fractured over Project C. To those who were willing to wait and see, Bevel's proposal to incarcerate kids rather than adults seemed not just unnecessary and stupid, but immoral.

King wasn't willing to wait and see, but he also rejected Bevel's strategy. Enlisting children was too dangerous. Another minister, Reverend Harold Long of the First Congregational Church, was appalled that Bevel was encouraging kids to disobey their parents and the law. A. G. Gaston exclaimed, "As a responsible citizen of Birmingham, I deplore the invasion of our schools to enlist students for demonstrations during school hours."

Shuttlesworth countered, "Sometimes you have to raise them so they'll be people on their own… [T]he best education was being

PETITION FOR PERMIT

TO: The City Commission of the City of Birmingham
The Honorable Albert Boutwell and The City Council of
City of Birmingham,
The Honorable Judson Hodges, City Clerk of the City of Birmingham,
The Honorable Ben Robinson, Traffic Engineer of the City of Birmingham:

This petition is addressed separately to each of the above city official bodies and officials because of the uncertainty petitioner has concerning which of these bodies or officials has authority to and actually does issue permits of the nature here requested. Furthermore, there is an additional uncertainty on the part of petitioner whether a permit is required by law for the type of activity which it desires to conduct for the reason that petitioner does not believe that it is a ~~march~~ *Parade* within the terms of Section 1159, of the Code of the City of Birmingham. Nevertheless, out of an abundance of caution and for the reason that petitioner desires to comply with the law, petitioner submits this application.

Petitioner desires on Wednesday, May 2, 1963 or Thursday, May 3, 1963, whichever date is more convenient for the City of Birmingham, to walk with a group of persons, two abreast, on the sidewalk, obeying all traffic regulations, beginning on Sixth Avenue and Sixteenth Street, North, at approximately 11:00 A. M., up Sixth Avenue to 19th Street, then on 19th Street to the City Hall, and there conduct a brief prayer meeting. En route ~~petitioners~~ *The Walkers* will block no doors, exits nor sidewalks. They will return via the same route. Petitioner respectfully requests reply to this petition by Tuesday, April 30, 1963, so that it may make plans accordingly. Please reply to the undersigned.

Rev. F. L. Shuttlesworth
505½ North 17th Street
Birmingham, Alabama
On behalf of Petitioner,
Alabama Christian Movement for
Human Rights.

the purpose of this walk is to symbolize opposition to racial segregation

educated to destroy the system which kept them enslaved." He had raised his own children this way. Six years earlier, while riding by themselves on an interstate bus from an integrated summer camp in Tennessee back to Alabama, Pat, Ricky, and Fred Jr., aged eleven through fifteen, refused to move when the driver ordered them to sit in the back of the bus. The children spent a night in the Gadsden City Jail. When their father drove to pick them up, local police ticketed him at every stop sign, even though he obeyed the traffic laws, and he lost his driver's license for a year.

In a nonviolence workshop at the end of April, Shuttlesworth spoke to the aspiring activists, saying, "You are soldiers, and you live in America, and nobody can tell you not to march." Meanwhile, he prepared a request for a permit "to walk with a group of persons, two abreast, on the sidewalk," on May 2 or May 3, "whichever is more convenient for the City of Birmingham." He didn't believe a permit was necessary but applied anyway "out of an abundance of caution and…to comply with the law." He also didn't know who had the authority to grant a permit, so he sent the request to all three commissioners, Mayor Boutwell, and two other city officials.

Many children were ready to go. Gwen Cook said that they didn't care that "[a] lot of people were worried we were going to get hurt. The reality of it was we were born black in Alabama. And we were going to get hurt if we didn't do something."

Still, King was not convinced. Bevel confronted him with a simple question: how old does a child need to be to accept Christ and join a church? As a Baptist minister, King knew the answer: age didn't matter as long as the child made a conscious decision. So, Bevel continued, how could King allow a child to commit to being a Christian but not allow that child to protest segregation? King agreed with the principle but still could not agree to funnel black children into Birmingham's jails.

Bevel knew King needed foot soldiers to parade to jail. "How I fill the jail is my business," he decided. Anyway, there was no choice. "We got to use what we got," Shuttlesworth pointed out.

"D-DAY" MINUS TWO AND COUNTING

On Tuesday, April 30, the city denied Shuttlesworth's petition to march on May 2 or 3. Students who had been participating in nonviolence workshops handed out hundreds of leaflets at the black high schools. (These had been secretly copied overnight, by candlelight, by a black printer who worked in a white-owned shop.) The leaflets urged students to leave school on Thursday, May 2, and march anyway, even without a permit.

At the mass meeting Tuesday night, Bevel called from the pulpit, "It will be our town that day. The only way to get what we want is for everybody to get together and tell Boutwell what we want." Cheers and "amens" erupted from the assembled. He called the day, "D-Day" after the invasion that helped the Allies win World War II.

The next day, May 1, Bevel hit the elementary schools with William Dothard, a local Movement organizer. Dothard, who had already been arrested twice, called himself "Meatball" to protect his and his parents' identities. At a mass meeting that night, Bevel promised, "We are going to break Birmingham wide open…[landing] where they least expect us… [We are] going to give the employees of the Negro schools a holiday tomorrow because the students are going to march." The D-Day march was on.

King remained uncertain about using kids. But at the end of the meeting, when he asked for volunteers to go to jail the next day, the adults stayed glued to their pews. "Nobody stood up but us kids," Gwendolyn Sanders said. Urging them to sit down, King tried to explain that jail was no place for children. After all, he had recently been released from "the utter darkness…in such a dungeon."

But they kept standing. "It was something that the children took hold to and wouldn't let go," Arnetta said.

AUDREY, JAMES, WASH, AND ARNETTA: MAY 1, 1963

At the youth meeting the night before, Audrey "just got up and walked down the aisle… After the mass meeting, I told my mother, 'I want to go to jail,' and she just said, 'OK.'"

Having watched whites pelt black adults and college students with eggs and ketchup at lunch counters, James knew he couldn't sit-in. But he could march.

Arnetta realized her parents were wrong. She hadn't yet done her part.

Wash wondered why on earth he should go to jail, voluntarily, without having done anything wrong.

Shuttlesworth later admitted, "When we retired for the night, we didn't know what we were going to do. We were at odds. Nobody could agree that children ought to be a major part of this."

However, hundreds of children—like Arnetta—had already signed the Ten Commandments of Nonviolence.

"It was too late for the conversation [the grown-ups] were having," high schooler Carolyn Maull said. "The ball had already started rolling."

CHAPTER EIGHT

Marchers leave Sixteenth Street Baptist Church, 1963

MAY 2.
D-DAY

"THERE'S GONNA BE A PARTY AT THE PARK"

MOST MORNINGS, young people who set their radio dial on WENN might wake up to the popular black DJ Shelley Stewart warbling, "Good goobly woobly!" Or, maybe they'd hear him cry, "Timberrrr, let it fall!" as he dropped a needle onto a spinning James Brown or Sam Cooke platter. On the morning of Thursday, May 2, however, his teenage listeners heard, "Kids, there's gonna be a party at the park. Bring your toothbrushes because lunch will be served."

Stewart's white fans must have wondered what he meant. The black ones got it. This was the signal to launch demonstrations in Kelly Ingram Park, down the street from the station's offices. They knew there was no more chance of getting lunch in the park than there was of being served a banana split at the counter at J. J. Newberry's. But they needed their toothbrushes because, after demonstrating, they would probably be going to jail—possibly for days.

Many kids headed straight to Sixteenth Street Baptist Church that morning without bothering to go to school first. James drove there with friends.

71

Audrey's parents took her after she said goodbye to her teacher and grandparents. Wash, as usual, was AWOL from school, but he didn't go to the church.

Other kids showed up at school and then left as soon as they got the word from march organizers or student leaders. As one of those leaders, Arnetta had learned at the mass meeting the night before that organizers wanted the kids to report to school first. Organizers thought it would make a better impression if student leaders didn't skip school the entire day, and they could persuade even more children to participate.

The leaders were assigned to visit specific classrooms. "We never entered into the classroom," high schooler Gwendolyn Sanders explained. "We would pass by the door…and give a cue, and the next thing you know, they were following us because the word was out that we were going to turn the school out that day… We knew which door to take them out, which route to take to the destination."

At Wenonah Junior High, guys walked up and down the hallways, calling students to come out. Kids at another school listened for Shelley Stewart to use the signal "hayride." At Parker High School, the signal was "sock hop." An organizer also stood across the street from Parker, holding a sign that read, "It's Time." R. C. Johnson, the principal, had heard rumors of a mass exodus and had padlocked the gates, probably violating the fire code. But kids squeezed through or climbed over the gates or slid out of windows. Music students in the Choir Annex simply ran out the back door.

When Arnetta saw Hosea Williams, one of her nonviolence trainers, arrive at her school, she thought, "It's here, it's about to happen!" She was joyful at "seeing all those children coming out to participate in the Movement." She described Dr. Bell, the principal of Ullman, as "running around like a chicken with his head cut off."

Under orders from Superintendent Theo Wright, principals read a notice warning students that, if they left school, they would be disciplined. They left anyway, in droves.

Teachers who were concerned about students' safety or who disapproved of their playing hooky tried to bar classroom doors. "A number of teachers told us we were wrong," Arnetta said, "that we were breaking laws, and we were putting our parents' jobs in jeopardy." But, her favorite teachers, Miss Woolfolk and Mrs. Cleopatra Goree, turned around and looked at the blackboard as if they didn't notice the students leaving their classrooms.

Miss Woolfolk thought that her students were doing the right thing. "I was teaching American Government, what the Constitution guarantees, what democracy should be about," she said. "And sitting in a segregated school system and going to the back door of restaurants—it made sense for students to take a stand."

"THE MORE WE WALKED, THE MORE YOU GATHERED"

After defying attendance rules and pouring out of school buildings all over the city, the students started walking to Kelly Ingram Park. Twenty kids from Fairfield—almost nine miles from downtown Birmingham—packed into an organizer's open convertible. Hundreds walked behind, as if they were following a float in a homecoming parade. Andrew Marrisett, a Movement organizer who didn't get a ride, said, "I had a Chevrolet on my right foot and one on my left."

As they passed other schools, some shouted, "Demonstration!" More kids ran out to join them. Masses converged on Sixteenth Street Baptist Church from all directions. "The more we walked, the more you gathered," Gwen Cook said. "We poured into Sixteenth Street like a waterfall."

Organizers directed some marchers to the Metropolitan AME Zion Church on the other side of the park. A third group congregated inside the Apostolic Overcoming Holiness Church of God on Seventeenth Street.

By the time Audrey and her parents arrived at Sixteenth Street Baptist, hundreds of kids were filling the sanctuary and the basement social hall. More kept coming—and more and more. As each group burst in, they shouted the name of their school to the raucous cheers of kids already there. Most of all, they sang: "Ain't Gonna Let Nobody Turn Me Round," "Oh, Freedom," "Keep Your Eyes on the Prize." Every song ratcheted up their fervor and reminded them why they were daring to confront the dreaded Birmingham police force and why they really did want to go to jail. "It was like one big pep rally," a student said.

Audrey talked quietly with her mother and father. As far she could tell, she was the youngest child there, and she didn't know anyone else. "My girlfriend…was to demonstrate, too, that day," she said. "I had expected to see her. But she wasn't there." Nevertheless, Audrey said, "I didn't have any fear."

"YOU ARE FREEDOM FIGHTERS… BUT WITHOUT WEAPONS"

Around noon, Shuttlesworth and Bevel called James and some other students aside for a meeting. Shuttlesworth reminded them, "[you are] freedom fighters, as much as those in the army. But without weapons… Still, you are expected to be as disciplined as soldiers."

"They asked us if we had any weapons," James said. "They passed the basket around… Nobody put anything in… They said, 'We're going to pass the basket around again. Because, if you don't go along with [nonviolence] totally, then don't go at all.' They passed the basket again." This time, James dropped his fingernail clippers into the basket. After the second circuit, he said, "It was full with pocketknives; somebody had brass knuckles, any little thing that people thought would give them an edge... We didn't know if we were going to be mixed with the jail population. So you're wondering how you're going to fit in with the guys who have been in there twenty years. There were a lot of unanswered questions."

Meanwhile, organizers asked children for their vital statistics—name, age, parents' names, and address. In case of emergency, they had to know whom to contact. Shortly before one o'clock, organizers arranged the eight hundred or so young demonstrators into groups of fifty, each group in double-file lines. There were so many that some gathered upstairs in the sanctuary and others in the basement. They were reminded of their destination—city hall—and their route. Some kids were handed signs to carry: "I'll Die to Make This Land My Home," "Justice for All. Now." "Can a Man Love God and Hate His Brother?"

In the basement, Audrey held her sign in one hand and clutched her board game in the other.

Arnetta waited by the door.

James stood upstairs at the very front of all the marchers, next to his friend Gertrude. "We were thinking about the seriousness of what we were about to do," he said.

At one o'clock, a DJ at WENN dropped the needle on the gospel song "All Men Created by God." This was the cue to start the march. The double doors of Sixteenth Street Baptist swung open.

James immediately saw the trouble they were about to step into.

"WE DIDN'T DISPERSE"

"When the door was opened, I was shocked at the number of people," he said. Beyond sawhorse barricades that surrounded the church, policemen sat at attention on motorcycles. Hundreds of black adults crowded the park. "I could see reporters... I remember hearing a man saying, 'They're coming out! They're coming out!' There were lights and people all around."

James knew the route that he and Gertrude and the forty-eight marchers behind them were to take to try to reach their destination, city hall, four blocks away. "We walked down the steps, turned left, and went up...Sixth Avenue," he said. "We crossed Seventeenth Street, and we started up the hill. We got about a block and a half until we were confronted."

Jamie Moore, the police chief who reported directly to Bull Connor, held up a huge bullhorn and stepped in front of James and Gertrude. "Stop!" Moore ordered. He told the marchers they were parading without a permit.

From behind him, James heard someone say he had a permit. "So, Gertrude and I are thinking, 'Why didn't they tell us?' It [turned out it] was somebody's driving permit," he said. "We answered, 'No. We do not have a permit.' We did not want to antagonize them." Then, said James, Moore threatened, "'If you do not disperse, you will be arrested.' Well, we didn't disperse."

At that point, things got even scarier for the marchers. Connor rolled up in a massive white car shaped and outfitted like a tank, complete with gun turrets. "Connor told them to arrest [us]," James said. "We were crammed into the paddy wagons that were meant to hold maybe eight people at the most—two in [each of] the four cubicles that they had. They crammed three and four of us into one cubicle and they continued to press the door until they got it shut and locked and [had] us taken off to jail."

As soon as James's group was hauled away, Bevel released the next group of fifty students. When that batch was arrested, the next group burst from the church.

"Leaving out of the basement...we had our signs and all, I started crying," Arnetta said. This time she didn't cry out of fear. "When I looked up and saw all of the people...the idea of what was about to take place. The...Movement was moving forward. It was just overwhelming."

Each group emerged singing and clapping. Audrey's group sang "Ain't Gonna Let Nobody Turn Me 'Round." She later exclaimed, "The singing was like a jubilance." Her group didn't march as far as James's had. "We got across the street, to the middle of the next block." As her parents watched, she was arrested and put in the paddy wagon. Holding her game tightly, she was driven to Juvenile Hall at City Jail.

Each time the last marcher in a group was loaded into a paddy wagon, the police assumed the parade was over. Just that morning, Connor had assured his men that King would quickly "run out of niggers." But, then the church doors would open again, and more kids would burst out. One officer finally asked Shuttlesworth, "How many more have you got?"

"At least a thousand," he answered, exaggerating the number.

"God A'mighty," the policeman exclaimed.

When they couldn't cram any more kids into paddy wagons, police commandeered school buses. The children climbed aboard as if they really were going to a party in the park. They happily waved their arms out of the bus windows.

The kids were exhilarated; the policemen were exhausted. An officer asked a marcher, "When is this going to end?" She responded, "Do we have our freedom yet?"

"I wish you could have your freedom just to stop this," he admitted.

Only one group reached city hall before being arrested. Nevertheless, the Movement reached its real destination—jail. By the end of Thursday, May 2, between five and eight hundred young people were incarcerated. This was two or three times the number of adults who had been arrested during the entire month of April.

Two thousand people jammed Sixteenth Street Baptist Church in celebration that evening. King intoned, "I have been inspired and moved today. I have never seen anything like it... If they think today is the end of this, they will be badly mistaken." James Farmer of the Congress of Racial Equality added, "This is the fight that decides whether America will live or die. Never before in any city has there been a movement so great."

Bevel asked everyone who felt inspired by the Movement to raise their hands. Hundreds of people's hands shot up. He told them to "go to jail... Let's all meet at the Sixteenth Street Church Friday, Saturday, and Sunday mornings and go from there to freedom."

77

Children wait to board the school bus that will take them to jail, 1963

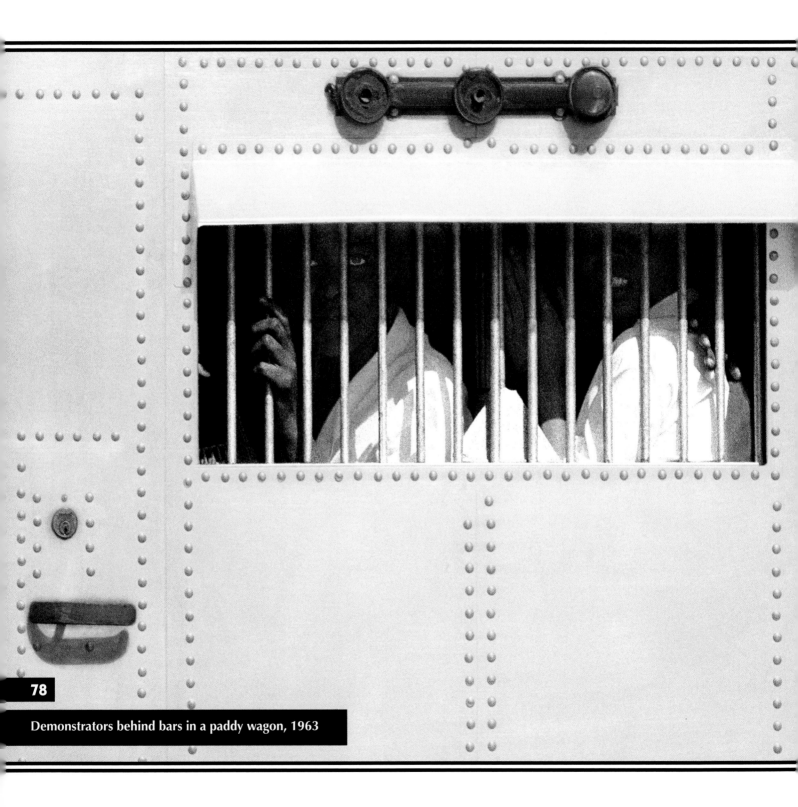

Demonstrators behind bars in a paddy wagon, 1963

Arnetta didn't go to the mass meeting that night. She was disappointed she hadn't been arrested. Somehow, she had gotten separated from the rest of the Peace Ponies, many of whom did get arrested and jailed. Instead, she went home and talked with her parents about the excitement of marching. They repeated their advice: "You've done your part. You need to leave this alone."

Audrey and James didn't go to the mass meeting either. They were in jail.

Audrey was taken to a large dayroom. She didn't know anyone, and everyone was older. Dinner was unappetizing. "They gave us grits…" she said. "They were horrible—all soupy, no salt." That night, she slept on a bunk bed "on one mattress, with one sheet," and no covers.

James's parents found out he was in jail by watching the news. His father and uncle were attending a medical convention in St. Louis. When they turned on the television in their hotel room, the newscasters were reporting the Birmingham arrests. James's uncle pointed at the screen and said, "Isn't that James right there?" Dr. Stewart immediately called his wife, who was at home.

Slow and resigned, she said, "I know, I know. I am looking. I see him." James said that his family wasn't surprised. "They knew that I was going to the Movement… I think they kind of knew that I would go [to the march]."

Meanwhile, Wash had arrived at Kelly Ingram Park to watch. "[W]e saw those people willingly turn themselves over to the police…," he said. His reaction: "Wow, they must be crazy." Experience had taught Wash that "the police was vicious murderers." He knew how much pain they could inflict on young black bodies—as Arnetta discovered the next day.

CHAPTER NINE

Marchers wait to be arrested, 1963.

MAY 3.
DOUBLE D-DAY

"YOU WONDERED HOW PEOPLE COULD BE
SO CRUEL."

"LET 'EM HAVE IT!"

ARNETTA WAS ONE of almost two thousand kids who played hooky from school on Friday, May 3, which Bevel dubbed Double D-Day. Most of them congregated at Sixteenth Street Baptist Church. They were anxious to rock and roll out the doors, down the steps, across the park, and into the school buses that would carry them to jail, where they would join the hundreds of kids who had been arrested the day before.

But first they were given their marching orders. These were especially important that day because firemen with trucks and hoses had joined the policemen opposite the church. Arnetta knew from her nonviolence training what that meant: the authorities were threatening to blast them with high-powered water hoses.

A group of twenty or so students was to head west, in the opposite direction from where most had marched the day before. They were decoys; their goal was to confuse the police and lure them from their posts. Sixty more students would take advantage of the gap in the police lineup and march eastward toward city hall.

Inside the church, marchers provided their vital statistics to organizers, who also collected half a trash can full of knives, nail files, scissors, and any other item that police might label a weapon. Dr. King gave them a pep talk. "If you take part in the marches today you are going to jail, but for a good cause." At one o'clock, they lined up. The doors opened, and they sashayed out, singing, "Free-ee-ee-dom. Free-ee-ee-dom. Free-ee-ee-dom. Freedom. Freedom" to the melody of "A-a-a-men."

For nearly an hour, everything proceeded according to plan. The westbound decoys surged around a policeman who tried vainly to halt them. The main group marched as far as the informal boundary between the black and white downtowns, where they were confronted by a blockade of squad cars and fire engines.

But Bull Connor hadn't planned on jailing two thousand more demonstrators that day. He was already running out of cells—just as organizers had intended. Young people kept pouring out of the church with no end in sight. All he could think to do was scare them into staying inside the church.

Connor and Police Captain Glenn V. Evans stepped in front of the group that was approaching Seventeenth Street and Fifth Avenue North. Several firemen hefted a massive hose equipped with the usual fogger nozzle and pointed it at the marchers.

"Disperse or you're going to get wet," Evans warned.

The marchers did not disperse.

"Let 'em have it!" Connor ordered.

The surge of water shocked most of the marchers into retreating. Several, though, faced the hoses and kept singing. "Free-ee-ee-dom. Free-ee-ee-dom."

The firemen escalated the barrage. By joining two hose ends to one nozzle mounted on a sturdy tripod, they could blast water through monitor guns at twice the force— 100 pounds per square inch instead of 50. They fixed their sights on the group marching up Eighteenth Street. Arnetta and another Peace Pony led this group.

The Peace Ponies had learned in nonviolence workshops how to protect themselves from the hoses: put their hands over their heads, roll into a ball. But "the little bit of training that we had did no good," Arnetta said. "[We were] hugging together, and the water just washed the two of us down the street. The water was piercing."

Some students thought they might die. "Once that water...hit me," Gwendolyn Sanders said, "I didn't know if I was going to survive it or not because the pressure from that hose was so great that it would knock your breath away."

The impact sheared the hair off the side of Carolyn Maull's head. It slammed another girl into a car, cutting her face. It lifted a boy

into the air. Screaming and shouting, the children didn't know which way to run as the firemen swept the hoses back and forth across the park. Dogs barked and yelped, seemingly desperate to get at them. A few marchers huddled in doorways or behind trees. Others were hurled against rough brick buildings. Dozens wrapped their arms around each others' shoulders to hold themselves up, though they soon crashed to the pavement. "You wondered how people could be so cruel," high schooler Rickey Powell said.

Arnetta's parents saw it all. "My daddy and mother, a lot of adults, came around… Little did my daddy know I was participat-ing. When my daddy saw the firemen putting water on me, he got upset," she recalled. "He was going to go…turn the water off. My mother, she was struggling with him to keep him from going over there. They would have killed him. That's what she told me… 'You could have gotten your father killed.'"

Her parents collected her and took her home, sopping wet and bruised. She put on dry clothes. Then, determined to go to jail, she told them she wanted to go back. Even though her parents were worried about her safety and distressed that she hadn't told them she planned to march, they reluctantly drove her back to the church.

83

Wash skipped school again that morning. Lured by the clamor, he dashed down Sixth Avenue North toward the marchers. "[I] stood on the street between the shotgun houses," he said, "and I watched them [the children] being manhandled by the police." He couldn't bear to stand by and do nothing.

Wash had never gone to nonviolence training, and there was no one to restrain him. Hiding behind rows of bystanders, he scooped up a handful of stones and hurled them at the police and firemen. Others joined him. Soon, rocks, bricks, and broken bottles—some flung from rooftops—crashed around the officers. "We would throw a brick, a bottle, and then we'd take off," Wash said. "That's what we were doing while everybody else was peacefully marching—looking for opportunities to strike a blow. We were more interested in hitting the policemen in the head with a rock than in going to jail."

When he saw an opportunity to save someone, though, Wash dared to come out into the open. "Somebody in the crowd threw a bottle," he said. "The policeman saw where it came from and came running into the crowd. The person who threw it took off. The crowd just split. When the policeman got to me, I tripped on purpose. And he tripped over me. He jumped up and kept going after the kid but the kid got away. I was so proud of myself."

Under attack, the firemen turned their hoses on the taunting crowd of about a thousand adults, who also refused to disperse. Audrey's mother worked in a nearby office; when a torrent of water shattered a window by her desk, she was stunned. "Don't cry," her boss said. "That's what they want."

Despite the flying bottles and surging water, young people kept emerging from the church. "No one should think that it was easy," Gwendolyn said. "No one should think that no one was frightened." But fear did not deter them. Instead of a walk in the park and a bus ride to jail, as they had expected, the teens marched directly into a melee.

Connor bolted the doors to Sixteenth Street Baptist Church from the outside, locking the five hundred to one thousand remaining marchers inside. Then he called for the K-9 unit.

Eight surging, snarling German shepherds—each on a short leash clenched by a policeman—tore across the park toward the protesters. Hundreds of terrorized bystanders screamed and fled.

Fifteen-year-old Walter Gadsden, a sophomore at Parker High School, had come to the park to check out the commotion. He was just turning to leave when, he said, "an officer grabbed me and held me while he turned a dog on me." The German shepherd lunged at his stomach. Fortunately, Walter suffered only a torn sweater and a bad scare. Like those who had come to march,

he was charged with parading without a permit and jailed in the same cell as James. Three other teens were bitten so badly—one by the biggest, blackest, meanest dog Arnetta had ever seen, a dog his handler named "Nigger"—that they had to be hospitalized. Also hospitalized were two firemen and a photographer who had been struck by bricks.

Dog attacks Walter Gadsden, 1963

Bevel grew worried. If demonstrators or bystanders became more aggressive, Connor would have an excuse to retaliate with even more violence, possibly something worse than hoses and dogs. The commissioner had already complained that the dogs weren't vicious enough.

As a result, two hours after that day's marches began, organizers decided to clear out troublemakers like Wash. Bevel borrowed a megaphone and joined the police in ordering everyone to go home. A fireman agreed to unlock the church doors if the protesters would leave quietly. The young people, including Arnetta, filed out. She would have to wait for yet another day to do her part to fill the jails.

Movement organizers got more than they bargained for that day. An additional five to eight hundred children were jailed, but also a number were injured, and many more, terrified. Blacks who had opposed the marches might have reacted by demanding they cease. Instead, in many cases, the violence against the marchers made them reconsider their position. A. G. Gaston, for instance, was just telling David Vann over the phone that he wished SCLC would leave town when he looked through his office window and saw a young girl deluged by hoses. Gaston abruptly changed his mind. "My people are out there fighting for their lives

and my freedom," he said. "I have to go help them." The events of Double D-Day accomplished what no earlier efforts had been able to do: unite black Birmingham. Many blacks finally agreed that any peaceful means to integrate the city was justified, including letting young children get jailed.

When video of children being hosed across asphalt and charged by growling dogs appeared on the news that night, America started to pay attention to how Birmingham treated its Negro population. One child was photographed holding up a hand-lettered sign that read, "We're Human, Too." But Connor didn't care about public opinion in the rest of America. His concern was public safety in Birmingham, and he intended to suppress anything that threatened it.

"I'LL LEAVE YOU HERE"

"Who forced you to march?"

"Why would you do this?"

"Are you against the American government?"

Audrey sat on a straight-backed chair in an otherwise vast, empty room, dressed in a pinafore and Mary Janes with turned-down socks. She looked across a broad conference table at five white men. She wondered if they planned to kill her.

"Nobody forced me," she answered politely.

"Are you sure?"

"Yes, sir. I decided myself."

"Why?"

"I want my freedom."

"What do you talk about at those meetings?"

"Our freedom. We want to be able to go places and do things like anybody else."

"Did you talk about Hitler?"

Audrey had never heard of Hitler.

"What about Communism?"

Audrey had never heard of that either.

"Are you against America?"

"No, sir."

Today, when people suspected of committing a crime are arrested, police must read them their Miranda rights. These rights allow the accused to remain silent while being questioned until they get advice from a lawyer. But *Miranda v. Arizona,* the Supreme Court case that granted these rights, was not decided until three years after Audrey was arrested, which meant that neither she nor the other children had any rights.

Audrey was frightened only two times during the week she spent in Juvenile Hall. The first time was during this interrogation. The second time, a matron snatched her from her seat and dragged her into a completely black room. "I told you to sit down," the matron snapped. "When I tell you something, you do it. Or I'll leave you here."

Audrey hadn't heard anyone order her to sit down. She was absorbed in playing her board game with another child in the dayroom. For failing to sit, she was threatened with solitary confinement, though the matron did not leave her alone there, after all. When Audrey returned to the dayroom, she put her game away, lay down her head, and cried.

"THERE'S NOBODY HERE WHO CAN SAVE YOU"

James, Gertrude, and other young people were crammed into paddy wagons and driven straight to jail. "My head was pressed up close to a bar," James said. "The driver jerked on the brake. My head bumped into the bars. I had a big knot on my head. He made it clear that we had entered hell, and he had the keys."

There were no television cameras to record or publicize what would happen to them there. James realized "there's nobody here who can save you... Fear began to really, really set in."

While being booked, he watched a policeman ask a friend his name. The friend responded with the phrase he had learned in nonviolence training: "No comment."

The officer, James said, "jumped up with such anger that the chair fell flat on its back on the floor as he lunged for the boy. He grabbed him in the collar and pulled him over the desk and onto the floor. He told him that he would lock him away where nobody would ever find him, and that went for the rest of us if we said 'no comment.' So, then the policeman gets up, straightens the chair, straightens the desk, and he looks at me and says, 'Now, what is your name?'"

James Stewart, fifteen, answered, "My name is John Davis. I'm sixteen." He made up names for his parents, too. He threw out "so much erroneous information so quickly, the officer said, 'Slow down, boy, slow down.'" The officer wrote it all down, then searched James and confiscated his fountain pen and watch. James had cleverly hidden a small transistor radio in his coat pocket, though, and had draped his coat over his arm before he reached the desk. The policeman neglected to search his coat.

After the interview, James said, "they put us in a holding facility that should have held maybe thirty people… They put close to three to four hundred boys in the same room. When they brought more, we were saying, 'You can't put more. There's no place to put them.' When they couldn't get the cell door open, they would reach in with a chain, and they would start hitting people with the chain to make them back up."

Like Audrey, James found the food repulsive. "You had grits on the bottom, water on top of the grits, and grease on top of the water," he said. "No salt, no seasoning. It was just not edible." James subsisted on occasional Three Musketeers candy bars secretly supplied by jail trustees—black inmates incarcerated for other crimes. James figured that they had access to vending machines.

On May 3, James's second day in jail, he listened to the news on his radio and heard something about water hoses. Soon after, new protesters arrived—and they were soaking wet. They told those who had been jailed on D-Day about the monitor-gun hoses. James learned about the dog attacks when some inmates asked him to help a young man who'd been severely bitten. The authorities, James said, "didn't take care of this guy. He was just in there with us with the holes in his leg. I looked at his leg. He was pretty seriously injured."

James asked them, "Why are you bringing him to me?"

They said, "Because your daddy is a doctor." But James couldn't help him.

"WE MUST NOT BOO THE POLICE"

Despite the mistreatment that the young demonstrators endured, the ministers at Friday night's mass meeting in Sixteenth Street Baptist Church did not criticize the Birmingham police force. On the contrary, referring to rock-throwers like Wash, Andrew Young scolded, "We have a nonviolent movement but it's not nonviolent enough... We must not 'boo' the police when they bring up the dogs—we must praise them."

Then, King reassured hundreds of worried parents. "Your daughters and sons are in jail... Don't worry about them. They are suffering for what they believe, and they are suffering to make this nation a better nation."

CHAPTER TEN

Ku Klux Klan members with children

VIEWS FROM OTHER SIDES

"THEY HATED US SO MUCH"

JAMES HADN'T TRULY UNDERSTOOD the Birmingham police force's capacity for torment until he was jammed standing-room only, alternately sweating and chilled, into a jail cell. He was a straight-A student and the son of professional parents; his experiences had been very different from Wash's. "I was shocked," James said, "that they were doing that; that they were in authority; that they hated us so much. They didn't even know us."

Why were the authorities so cruel? Why were white people so determined to keep blacks off their lunch counter stools and out of their schools and swimming pools? Why would they allow officials to imprison, interrogate, hose, and set vicious dogs on children?

"The great majority in Birmingham do not want integration," Connor asserted when the federal court ruled that segregation of public parks was unconstitutional. Because he and the Klan had thoroughly intimidated white people as well as black people, it's impossible to know what the majority of Birmingham's whites wanted. Few dared to contradict him.

91

Interviews with people who lived there in the 1960s and readings from other sources indicate a range of views, from the most brutally racist to the most daringly integrationist. Each person had her or his own way of expanding, maintaining, or tolerating—and occasionally bridging—two parallel, unequal Birminghams.

"YOU GOTTA KEEP YOUR WHITE AND YOUR BLACK SEPARATE!"

Many white people opposed integration because they firmly believed that the "white race" was superior to the "black race"—that whites were smarter, harder working, and more honest. A prominent lawyer said, "All

White students protest integration

of the Negroes in Alabama were all savages in Africa... They had no concept of working in order to obtain a livelihood. Their concept, when they were hungry, was to raid the jungles."

Reverend Joseph Ellwanger, a white civil rights activist, explained what the segregationists feared: "To break down the barriers of segregation is to permit...an inferior race to mix with a superior race, and the inevitable result would be...a mongrelization of and a pulling down of that white superior race... Many members of the KKK had that as almost a religious belief in their hearts, that we've got to maintain that kind of purity of the race or otherwise we're dooming ourselves and our future generations."

Most white children had no opportunity to learn that the idea of racial superiority is nonsense. They were raised with these sorts of convictions and were barred from interacting with anyone who might prove them wrong. "We were all anti-integration," Charles Entrekin, a white high school student at that time, later said about his neighbors. "You could walk down the street and knock on anybody's door and ask them if they were in favor of integration, and they would say, 'No, not at all.' You had a...uniformity of belief in the inferiority of the black race."

Diane McWhorter, a white girl a year older than Audrey, heard her father say, "the nigger is oriented to rote memory only." That is, he believed blacks could memorize facts but not think or analyze. Pam Walbert, also white and a year older than James and Arnetta, said her high school teacher taught the class that "it was proven that the blood of blacks ran in a more sluggish way than the blood of whites." The teacher told the class that this was why black students couldn't go to school with whites; they couldn't learn.

"THE RESULTS OF OUR LABOR"

Many Americans also worried that Russian revolutionaries were plotting to overthrow democracy. It was rumored that communists had secretly infiltrated all levels of the American government as well as political parties and social groups. Officials, journalists, and ordinary citizens accused anyone they mistrusted—for almost any reason, including questioning the city's Segregation Ordinances—of being a communist. If convicted, often with no evidence, citizens could lose their jobs or be imprisoned.

Fearmongers asserted that communism threatened not only democracy but also capitalism, the American economic system. Under segregation, most whites were

93

wealthier than most blacks, who generally worked at nonprofessional, low-paying jobs. They were the hired help—maids, custodians, ironworkers—holding jobs whites didn't want.

Reverend Abraham Lincoln Woods, Calvin Woods's brother, observed that whites "were enjoying the results of our labor... They were enriched. We were impoverished."

He was right. In 1960, the median income for Birmingham's wealthiest white families was $10,668. For its wealthiest black families, the median income was only $6,545.

Many whites feared that if the communists took over, the government would own everything and could hire blacks to do the jobs whites held, for less money. Charles heard his parents talk. "They were worried that whites were going to lose jobs to blacks," he remembered. Diane's father told her that white civil rights activists were spearheading the communist takeover of America—and, furthermore, they had cunningly duped gullible blacks into helping them.

94

A postcard identifying Martin Luther King Jr. as a communist

"I CANNOT CONDONE... THE USE OF CHILDREN"

Since whites rarely interacted with blacks other than those who worked as their servants, many might not have considered how they felt about integration. They didn't have to think about it because integration wasn't an option—until Shuttlesworth, King, and others insisted that it was not just an option but an absolute necessity. Suddenly, the white citizens of Birmingham had to face the possibility of sharing space with black people. But regardless of whether or not any whites would be willing to accept integration, many deplored the activists' techniques to achieve it.

On May 4, the *Birmingham News* reported that hundreds of children had "walked out of their classrooms...to become members of an undisciplined mob of demonstrators." Within days, as the newspaper described it, "thousands of Negro teen-agers broke through police and fire lines and flooded the downtown business district... [Y]elling and jeering Negroes broke and ran against traffic lights, in the middle of the street and through alleys...shoving white people off sidewalks, and bulling their way in and out of department stores." Shoppers stayed away; businesses suffered as sales plunged.

Mayor Boutwell spoke for many whites when he said, "I cannot condone and you cannot condone the use of children... I do not need to emphasize the difference between demonstrations by adults and the terrible danger of involving immature teen-agers and younger children."

At the national level, Attorney General Kennedy agreed. "An injured, maimed or dead child," he said, "is a price that none of us can afford to pay. School children participating in street demonstrations is a dangerous business."

"OUTSIDE AGITATORS"

Local citizens were especially outraged that "outside agitators," as they labeled people like King, Bevel, and Shuttlesworth, were stirring up trouble in their hometown. (Though Shuttlesworth was still deeply involved in the Birmingham Movement, he had moved to Ohio two years earlier for a better job. King was from Atlanta, and Bevel was from Nashville.) "We didn't think much of Martin Luther King," Charles said. "We thought he was fomenting problems."

Boutwell urged "local Negro citizens" not to follow "the questionable leadership of strangers, people whose sole purpose is to stir strife and discord here, and then who will leave our citizens to pay the penalty of

"All these years...there should have been social exchange between colored and white children... To me the solution is very simple: just treat human beings as human beings. But to many of these people Negroes are not human beings. Please don't use my name... If you do I will lose my job."

—Anonymous, high school teacher

"We've got to accept integration. Not that I want to but it is here."

—Jesse Madaris, parking lot attendant

"You can't blame the Negro for what they are trying to do. Sooner or later they are going to win, but they aren't going to school with my children."

—Tommy Arwood, auto body shop worker

"When a man takes small children and puts them where they can get hurt, he is far worse than Bull Connor."

—R. L. Burdette, scrap iron broker

this discord, once they have worked their mischief." Although almost all of the demonstrators and most of the leaders were from Birmingham, many whites agreed with the opinion of a white woman who demanded of a native teenage marcher, "Why don't you niggers go back to the North? The niggers here is satisfied."

Many white people condemned the chaos downtown and the alleged outsiders who instigated it. Some of them may have used their disapproval of the Movement's tactics as a cover for their racism and their desire to maintain segregation. Others might have been open to integration but truly detested the leadership's confrontational techniques and use of children. It's impossible to know how many whites in Birmingham fell into the first group, how many into the second, and how many somewhere in between. No one was taking polls to find out.

"AFRAID TO COME OUT IN THE OPEN"

A small but noticeable minority of whites quietly supported integration—or, at least, rejected hard-line segregation—in the voting booth. Although most whites voted for Connor in the runoff election in April, enough supported Boutwell that he and the new city council won. The day after the election, Reverend Ed Gardner, a black minister, pointed out, "Many white people living in Birmingham today are sympathetic with our movement," although, he added, most "are afraid to come out in the open."

Several white people had been working toward integration behind the scenes. Emil Hess, a department store owner, removed the colored drinking fountain and placed paper cups beside the white one for all of his customers. He also quietly desegregated the dressing rooms in his store. David Vann met with blacks to negotiate an end to the Selective Buying Campaign.

Even a few policemen objected to segregation or, in any case, objected to enforcing it. Police Chief Jamie Moore admitted that some of his officers "absolutely didn't like it. I mean they didn't like it." On D-Day, police officer Captain George Wall said to Captain Evans, "Ten or fifteen years from now, we will look back on this and we will say, 'How stupid can you be?'"

But everyone had to obey the Segregation Ordinances, even those who despised them. "The ultimate tragedy of Birmingham," King observed, "was not the brutality of the bad people but the silence of the good people."

"TRYING TO CHANGE THINGS"

A few white merchants came out into the open because they feared that the negative perception of Birmingham was bad for business. Though they supported segregation, they opposed Connor's tactics. The most prominent of these businessmen was Sidney Smyer, who had helped orchestrate the change in Birmingham's government in order to remove Connor.

Only a very few whites openly opposed segregation and dared to speak out loud. Reverend Ellwanger preached at mass meetings and helped the SCLC plan strategies. Eileen Walbert, Pam's mother, worked with the Birmingham Council on Human Relations, a biracial organization, to stop police violence against young black males and to remove "White" and "Colored" signs from drinking fountains and buses. "A few people," Mrs. Walbert said, "were trying to change things."

Whites who tried to improve race relations often suffered for their efforts. The Klan and the police sent informers to Council meetings. Klan members often followed the whites home in their cars, flashing high-beam headlights and nudging their bumpers. A newspaper published their photographs and addresses; neighbors yelled "Communists!" at them.

The Walberts once found a cross burning in their yard. Some people received threatening phone calls in the middle of the night. Ellen Cooper, whose father was a lawyer who represented black miners, knew not to answer the phone or the door when she was home alone. Lamar Weaver, a white minister and steelworker, helped Shuttlesworth integrate the white waiting room at the train station. The police threw him out of the station into the fists of a waiting mob, some of whom he recognized from work. He barely escaped to his car, which the mob bashed with cement blocks. He then raced to a black funeral home where the owner hid him in a coffin.

Others were affected professionally. When Pam's father, a music teacher, hung a picture of Martin Luther King Jr. over his piano, one of his students quit. Dale Russakoff's father, a doctor at the University of Alabama hospital, resigned when he was told that he could not require medical students to call black patients by their full, given names.

Trying to change Birmingham, especially out in the open, was very risky business. Charles said, "These people were heroes because they were standing up to speak out. They were the only little voices to counter a huge megaphone of popular news media."

"THERE'S TROUBLE DOWNTOWN"

While black teenagers were being arrested downtown, many white teenagers were unaware—not just of the protests, but also of their causes. Only when they left town did many of them understand the troubles at home.

"Culture is like weather," Charles said. "People breathe in the prejudices of their culture without any understanding of what they're taking in. It takes something to wake them up." Charles "woke up" in college and then had "tremendous fights" with his father, who called him "a traitor to his race" and threw him out of the house. "The waking up period was startling...," he said. "[W]e felt betrayed and lied to."

Pam had a friend who said the same thing after she sat in classrooms with black students at college in Ohio. She discovered they weren't inferior, after all. "It's like finding out that everyone you ever loved or respected had lied to you," she told Pam.

Many white families taught their children to believe they were better than blacks. Boys from such families would go "nigger-knocking in nigger-town" on Saturday nights—that is, driving through black neighborhoods to throw water balloons at the black residents or knock elderly black people over. Interviewed on a national television program, a local college student stated, "I don't believe in the mixing of the races, and I don't care what anybody says. I might be prejudiced. I don't know. I probably am… I am against integration."

Generally, though, race was not a topic of conversation in white households. Susan Levin, a white high school senior in 1963, said, "I was always aware that there were unpleasant things going on. I was equally aware that these were not things to be talked about. They were very dangerous… Nobody ever said to me, 'You can't talk about these things.'… Yet, somehow, we didn't."

Not even in early May 1963. When Susan's father told her, "There's trouble downtown. Don't go," she obeyed him. The "trouble" didn't touch her. Segregation so thoroughly cleaved blacks from whites within the city of Birmingham—and, furthermore, Birmingham from the rest of the country—that while thousands of young black people protested, thousands of young whites remained oblivious.

"A COTTON CURTAIN"

Today, with news streaming constantly on television, radio, the internet, and portable wireless devices, it's hard to imagine that many white people knew nothing about the demonstrations that consumed the area around Kelly Ingram Park. The media was very different then, and Alabama, along with the rest of the Deep South, was different from much of the rest of the country. "In Alabama," Wash said, "there was a cotton curtain. News didn't come in, and news didn't get out." One woman who worked in the Jefferson County Courthouse, where hundreds of teens, including Wash, were jailed, says she never saw or heard any young person arrested or incarcerated, never read about it, and never even knew it happened.

The two white-owned newspapers, the *Birmingham News* and the *Birmingham Post-Herald*, buried most articles and photos of the protesters on inside pages. It wasn't until Charles left home that he realized that these papers didn't cover news at all; they published popular opinion. "They weren't doing investigative reporting," he said. "The *New York Times* was writing revealing stories about what was going on in Birmingham but we weren't reading them."

Even the black-owned *Birmingham World* editorialized against the demonstrations. It published fewer articles and photos than the local white papers.

The three national television networks reported on the events, but their nightly news broadcasts lasted only fifteen minutes. Dale's father complained that he had to watch *The Huntley-Brinkley Report,* a national news program headquartered in New York City and Washington, DC, to find out what was happening right there in downtown Birmingham.

The *Birmingham News* continued to suppress the story for decades. In 2004, a researcher discovered a cardboard box in a closet. It was marked "Keep. Do Not Sell." Inside were thousands of unpublished, unseen photographic negatives of civil rights activities that took place in Birmingham between 1950 and 1965. "The editors thought if you didn't publish it, much of this would go away," a photographer explained. The publisher finally released some—but not all—of the photos in 2006.

"I FELT FLOODED WITH THE HOLY SPIRIT"

When Pam was ten, a neighbor made a racist comment while driving the carpool to school. Pam refused to ride with him ever again, even in pouring rain. When she was twelve, she told her sixth-grade class that blacks should be allowed to go to any school they want. "The teacher and everyone argued with me," Pam said. The next day, her teacher announced they would no longer discuss current events. Right then, Pam knew there was "a struggle going on, and I would be called upon to enter into it."

Pam was no less frightened of retaliation than any other white person. She saw the cross burning on her family's lawn and knew their phone was tapped. "I was often afraid," she admitted. "This cold kind of fear…would feel like my insides were turning to liquid; then, a hot spear. Then, I would turn cold and shiver."

Still, she couldn't stand the "apartheid" that defined Birmingham. "No matter how much we might wish otherwise, the black people were in this part of town, and the white people were in that part of town," she said. "This seemed so entrenched, I couldn't imagine it changing." After Shuttlesworth was beaten for trying to enroll his daughters in segregated Phillips High School, Pam wrote him a fan letter. "I told him how much I admired him, how much I wished that it would be possible for us to meet one day."

Her wish came true when she joined her parents at a meeting of the Council on Human Relations in the basement of Shuttlesworth's church. "There he was," she said, "coming down the aisle toward me with this beautiful grin." Pam cried. "Their words," she said about the ministers' sermons at the meeting, "were like sweet rain from heaven."

Soon after, Shuttlesworth invited her to come back for a youth fellowship meeting where black students who had been jailed and released were to be honored. She and the other two "nonprejudiced" high schoolers she knew attended.

"It was a very hot day, beastly and dusty in that part of town. There were some cans of soda there but they didn't have enough for everybody. We were sitting in a circle, and they started passing around a can of soda." Like other white kids, Pam had been taught at school that black people had a lot of diseases. "Even though I knew that wasn't true, I had never had the experience of sitting down with a group of young black people and eating together," she said. "They started passing this can of soda around the circle. I remember watching it being lifted to…a black girl's lips. At the moment when I lifted that can to my lips, I felt flooded with the Holy Spirit."

WHITE KIDS AND BLACK KIDS: FRIDAY, MAY 3, 1963

At about the same time:

Diane McWhorter was playing with her fifth-grade classmates (one of whom played Scout in the movie *To Kill a Mockingbird*) at the private Brooke Hill School; Audrey Hendricks was sitting in a juvenile detention center dayroom.

Charles Entrekin was pondering what to do after graduation; Washington Booker was throwing bricks at the police.

Susan Levin, who had recently decided which college to attend, was in class at Shades Valley High School; James Stewart was crammed into a jail cell.

Pam Walbert, who had recently won a scholarship in the Junior Miss Alabama competition, was rehearsing a theater production; Arnetta Streeter was getting pounded by water from a high-pressure hose.

CHAPTER ELEVEN

Protesters march down street in Birmingham, 1963

MAY 4-6, 1963

"DELIVER US FROM EVIL."

SATURDAY, MAY 4

"NOBODY ELSE WAS GETTING OUT"

AFTER THREE DAYS IN JAIL, James was starting to feel sick. His parents were trying to arrange his release, but James had given a fake name and address and claimed he was sixteen years old when he was booked. As a result, the family lawyer had been unable to locate him. "He had been looking for me some way," James said. "There were people who knew me, and finally the word got back that they were looking for *me!*"

James was tempted to leave jail when the lawyer showed up, but he refused. "[N]obody else was getting out and we understood that we would get out as a group," he explained. James and his fellow protesters believed that the Movement leadership would send an attorney to represent all of them, and he intended to stay until that happened. As the day wore on, more inmates, some sopping wet, were shoved into his cell.

Reverend A. D. King, one of the few adults arrested on D-Day, was in the same cell as James and the other three to four hundred young men. To keep their spirits up, James said, "He would sing sometimes for fifteen minutes by himself. He wouldn't give up. Eventually, one or two of us would begin to sing, and then we would all join in." One of James's favorite songs was "Everybody Loves Freedom."

Singing comforted the jailed protesters all over town. Shuttlesworth advised students, "when you're arrested, sing your hearts out!" In one jail, boys and girls in nearby cells took turns serenading each other. At another, when wardens sang "Dixie" over the loudspeaker system, students drowned them out, belting "We Shall Overcome."

"STROLLING NEGROES"

Movement strategists concocted a new plan to catch the police off guard that Saturday. On D-Day and Double D-Day, the marches had begun at exactly 1:00 p.m. and ended at 3:00 p.m. On Saturday, May 4, protesters started two hours earlier. At 11:00 a.m., small groups of teenagers, some wisely wearing raincoats in case they got hosed, ambled out of Sixteenth Street Baptist Church and Apostolic Overcoming Holiness Church of God. The teens meandered— apparently randomly—until about two-

dozen of them converged at a predetermined spot. One girl pulled out a banner she had hidden in her clothes that read, "Love God and Thy Neighbor." The entire group, holding the banner high, then marched over to city hall.

Just as they arrived, Connor stepped outside. He hadn't expected to face protesters for at least another hour. Connor had the students arrested. Grinning, they followed a policeman down a ramp into the station.

Meanwhile, several adults, including Mrs. Streeter's friend Mrs. Robey, drove about fifty other young people to the white downtown. Some whipped out picket signs. Surprised and irritated that the protesters were no longer confining themselves to the black part of town, Connor told his force to arrest all "strolling Negroes," who would then be ferried to jail on school buses. Once again, Connor ordered the doors of Sixteenth Street Baptist Church locked to prevent more protesters from hitting the streets.

A crowd of about three thousand adults had gathered in Kelly Ingram Park, where events turned nasty. The spectators hurled rocks and bottles at the police, and the police sprayed the crowd with hoses. No one knows who acted first. The result was another melee. Wash might have joined the bottle-throwing throng, except his mother

James Bevel consults with police, 1963

had taken him to spend the weekend with her family in Demopolis, about a hundred miles south of Birmingham.

Bevel grew concerned when he spotted guns and knives in the crowd. Borrowing a police captain's bullhorn, he bellowed, "Get off the streets now. We're not going to have violence. If you're not going to respect the policemen, you're not going to be in the Movement."

Stunned to hear him side with the police, the crowd dispersed. Bevel was equally surprised that they complied. "I'm with the police, talking through the bullhorn and giving orders, and everybody was obeying the orders," he said. "It was like, wow."

SHUTTLE DIPLOMACY

By mid-afternoon, tensions downtown subsided, but newspapers, magazines, and television displayed the shocking images of what had occurred. King had timed the protests to take advantage of the deadlines for the nightly news programs, and footage of kids crammed into paddy wagons and being washed down the street by fire hoses

HEADLINE NEWS

"Dogs and Hoses Repulse Negroes at Birmingham. 3 Students Bitten."
  —The New York Times, May 4, 1963

"Hoses Again Drive Off Demonstrators,"
  —The New York Times, May 5, 1963

"Sirens Wail, Horns Blow, Negroes Sing,"
  —The Birmingham News, May 7, 1963

"Alabama Negroes Defy Police and Block Town."
  —The Times of London, May 8, 1963

"Sospesa per un giorno l'agitazione dei negri antirazziali a Birmingham."
  —Italian newspaper, May 1963

were especially effective in rousing national outrage and attracting the attention of the federal government.

The federal government had not previously intervened, partly because federal law did not explicitly forbid private businesses, such as department stores and lunch counters, from maintaining segregated facilities. Also, the protests—sit-ins, for example—that had occurred on private property were illegal, and therefore the federal government was not required to intercede to protect the demonstrators.

Had they wanted to, the president and attorney general could have intervened on behalf of SCLC, ACMHR, and the marchers, since their picketing and marching took place on public property. However, the Kennedy brothers did not want to take sides. They were members of the Democratic Party, which was the most powerful party in the South. Most southern Democrats were committed to the idea of white supremacy, and the White House did not want to offend that branch of their party.

The president's spokesman stated that he hoped the situation would be resolved by the people of Birmingham. In short, as far as the federal government was concerned, what was happening in Alabama was Alabama's problem.

Still, President Kennedy admitted that a picture of a dog biting a young man made him feel sick, and he directed the U.S. attorney general to send a negotiator to Birmingham.

That afternoon, Burke Marshall, assistant attorney general for civil rights, arrived in Birmingham. He quickly noticed that "there were many whites that wouldn't talk to any blacks, and there were many more whites that wouldn't talk to certain blacks, and there were no whites…

who would talk with Martin King." Marshall would have to conduct "shuttle diplomacy," moving back and forth between groups instead of meeting with everyone together. But first, he had to figure out which black civil rights leaders and which white businessmen and politicians to involve.

Shuttlesworth didn't want anyone else—black or white—to speak for him. He wanted to talk directly to the white leadership. But few, if any, would agree to meet with him. Most white leaders also refused to allow anyone to represent them in negotiations. The dispute between Connor and Boutwell was still unresolved, and city leadership was in chaos, As a result, Marshall had to juggle not only blacks versus whites, but also blacks versus blacks and whites versus whites.

The chamber of commerce had established a Senior Citizens Committee, a group of eighty-nine of the city's most prominent merchants, industrialists, and other key professionals. (In this case, "senior" refers to important rather than elderly citizens.) This all-white group, selected by Sidney Smyer the previous summer, was assigned the colossal task of solving the city's race problems. Smyer, the committee's chair, was the only member who allowed himself to be publicly identified. The names of the other eighty-eight members were kept secret in order to protect their businesses and personal lives.

This committee formed a Biracial Subcommittee, which consisted of relatively open-minded white businessmen who were willing to sit down and negotiate with Negroes they deemed "responsible." Neither the identities nor the number of citizens who served on the Biracial Subcommittee was ever revealed.

AUDREY

While this political muddle tied up the city, Audrey, like James, passed her third day in detention on Saturday. "I didn't have any fresh underwear or a change of clothes or a toothbrush," she said. She shared a bathroom with fifteen to twenty other girls. During the day, they were allowed outside in a concrete recreation area but Audrey said, "we didn't do a lot of playing... There was no classes to keep up your academics. So you just were basically there." She was surprised the wardens hadn't made some sort of plans for them. Because of her experiences with the Movement, Audrey had assumed all adults were well organized.

SUNDAY, MAY 5

JAMES AND ARNETTA

On Sunday, Dr. and Mrs. Stewart sent their lawyer back to James's overcrowded cell with a message for him: "You need to come out."

Because the young prisoners' cell was packed so tight, most of them had been forced to stand—day after night, night after day. "We had to sleep in shifts," James said. "Certain ones would lie down and try to sleep, and the rest of us stood around the walls or sat in the windowsills... There were no chairs. And when we couldn't stand any longer, we would arouse them and have them stand up, and then we would sleep."

Even worse, "the toilet facilities were deplorable. At the end of this room, there were five toilet seats... You went to the bathroom in front of three to four hundred people." The ceiling over the toilets was open to the sky. When it rained, the water drenched them while they were going to the bathroom. As further punishment, he said, their jailors "turned the air conditioning on at night and the heat on during the day."

By his fourth day in jail, James was getting sick. "I was at my wits' end," he admitted. His parents provided bail—thirty dollars cash—for him as well as for three or four of his friends. As he left, "people put all kinds of notes on me," he said. "They... wanted me to call their mother...and tell them they were okay." The police returned his pen, but they had confiscated and kept his radio when they realized he was listening to the news. The minute James got home, he took a bath. Then, for the first time since Thursday morning, he ate something besides candy bars.

Meanwhile, Arnetta was still disappointed and frustrated that she hadn't been arrested with the other Peace Ponies. She yearned to try again, but Bevel had called off marches on the Sabbath.

"DAMMIT! TURN ON THE HOSES!"

Sunday blossomed into a day of miracles. In the morning, blacks held kneel-ins at a dozen white churches, a few of which welcomed them. Some white congregants shook hands with the protesters.

That afternoon, Guy and Candie Carawan were arrested on the steps of New Pilgrim Baptist Church. The Carawans, who were white, had composed many of the Movement's songs. They had hoped to record Sunday's mass meeting at the church for the Smithsonian Institution. But, Connor announced, "No blacks and whites would be singing together in Birmingham."

Bevel was so angered by their arrests that he called from the pulpit, "We're tired of this mess!" He wanted the congregation to protest but didn't want to break the Sunday truce. So he declared, "Let's not march. Let's just walk."

Over a thousand worshippers spontaneously rose from their pews, and, for the first time since Project C began, adults and children "walked" together. The line stretched five blocks long, forming the largest protest march in Birmingham history.

Led by New Pilgrim's Reverend Charles Billups Jr., the crowd sang "I Want Jesus to Walk with Me" and strode—in high heels and veiled hats, in suits and neckties—toward the Southside Jail, where they hoped to hold a pray-in. Inspired by the courage of the incarcerated young people, they risked arrest, job loss, and attacks by the police.

Two blocks shy of the jail, they were confronted by ranks of police and firemen, led by Connor. "You have no parade permit," he called. "Reverse your direction and return to the church... If you do not, then we will have no alternative but to disperse you in whatever way we can."

Reverend Billups called back, "Turn on your water, turn loose your dogs, we will stand here till we die." Tears ran down his face. Many of the assembled knelt and took up his chant.

"Turn on the hoses," Connor commanded. The firemen didn't move.

"Dammit! Turn on the hoses!" Connor repeated.

Still, the firemen didn't move. Instead, some of them cried. One fireman told his chief, "You turn it on yourself. I am not going to do that." Another said, "We're here to put out fires, not people." The firemen and policemen stepped aside to allow a thousand blacks singing "I Got Freedom Over My Head" to cross the street to a park, where they knelt and prayed.

Shuttlesworth likened the occasion to "the parting of the Red Sea." King called these "thirty seconds... one of the most fantastic events of the Birmingham story."

Miracle Sunday, as it came to be known, was not over yet. That evening, the white folksinger Joan Baez performed a free concert at all-black Miles College. In her perfect-pitch soprano, Baez hummed the melody of "We Shall Overcome" to simple guitar chords. She sang the first verse solo. Then the audience joined her for the remaining verses: "We'll walk hand in hand" and, louder, "We are not afraid." Applause and whistles reverberated in the hall.

Elsewhere that evening, Marshall met with the Biracial Subcommittee. The white department store owners indicated that they'd think about desegregating some fitting rooms. Neither of the two city governments, however, offered to meet any of ACMHR's other demands itemized in the Points for Progress.

Miracle Sunday offered hope, but no solutions. The marches would start up again the next day.

MONDAY, MAY 6

"HE DISRESPECTED HIM"

At nine o'clock Monday morning, James attended his court hearing. Because he'd given a false age when he was arrested, he was initially sent to an adult court.

"The judge called me up to verify my age. When I told him I was fifteen, he couldn't do anything with my case," James said.

"What are you doing here?" Judge Charles Brown demanded.

Arthur Shores was representing James. He stood to defend him. Brown peered down at Shores and commanded, "Sit down, Arthur."

The judge's order shocked James. "I was appalled at the way he disrespected him," he said. "So I said to myself, 'I'm pretty much on my own here.'... They called the

bailiff, and they took me straight over to juvenile detention. My parents and attorney had to go there to get me."

"I AIN'T SCARED OF YOUR JAIL"

At about the same time that James appeared for his first hearing, Mrs. Booker had a stern talk with her son. She and Wash had returned from Demopolis Sunday evening. Suspecting that Wash might play hooky from Ullman High again on Monday and throw more bottles at policemen around Kelly Ingram Park, she ordered him, "Don't you dare go down there."

She had good reason to worry. Connor had called in reinforcements from surrounding counties. Hundreds of officers with guns, clubs, and short-wave radios surrounded the park and surveyed the area from rooftops.

But Wash had no intention of obeying his mother. "When she took me to school Monday morning," he said, "I went straight through the school. In one door, right out the other. There must have been three to four hundred kids leaving the school, headed toward downtown."

Many had seen a flier that leaders had distributed to the black high schools. "Fight for freedom first, then go to school," it read. "Join the thousand in jail who are making their witness for freedom… It's up to you to free our teachers, our parents, yourself, and our country."

Wash didn't know what he would do when he reached the park but, he said, "I knew I was going back down there." So many of his friends had been arrested, he realized that "If you wanted to have folks to talk to and hang out with, you had to go to jail."

Wash joined the throng, which marched up Fourteenth Street South and crossed to Sixteenth Street. "When we got over the crest of the hill, we could see all the way down Sixteenth," he said. "And there was another group of kids coming from Carver [High School]. We saw them and started cheering. The next two blocks, we looked down Sixth Avenue [North], and there were kids coming from Parker [High School]. There was a big crowd of us. And we were all right there at Sixteenth. *And it was on!*"

The principal of Parker High tried to block students from streaming out of the school. As 1,300 of them swept past him, they chanted "Gotta go, Mr. Johnson, gotta go."

Fewer than nine hundred of Birmingham's almost 7,500 black high schoolers showed up at school. By nine a.m., two thousand of them had gathered inside Sixteenth Street Baptist Church, and at least one thousand more sweated in the ninety-degree heat outside. Joan Baez, who had been smuggled to the church facedown in the back seat of a car, joined the students inside.

Bevel proposed a deal with Police Chief Moore: if the students marched peacefully that afternoon, would officers arrest them without using hoses and dogs? Moore agreed, although he refused to shake on it when Bevel offered his hand. In case the blacks broke the deal, Connor yet again surrounded the park with fire engines and high-pressure hoses. Dr. King reminded the high-spirited youngsters, "The whole world is watching you."

As on previous days, organizers collected every item that resembled a weapon. Wash regretted having to relinquish his pocketknife and thought, "I should have left [it] at home."

Just after one o'clock, a group of sixty marchers emerged from the church and headed up East Sixth Avenue. They were led by Dick Gregory, a black comedian from Chicago, who carried a sign that read, "Everybody Wants Freedom." Immediately, forty policemen confronted him.

"Do you have a permit to parade?" a captain asked him.

"No," Gregory answered. (Not "No, sir," which was the way that blacks were expected to speak to whites.)

"No what?" the captain demanded.

"No. No. A thousand times No."

"I hereby place you all under arrest."

The crowd cheered. Kids pumped their arms, shimmied their legs, wagged their bottoms. To the melody of "The Old Grey Mare," they belted out these lyrics: "I ain't scared of your jail 'cause I want my freedom, want my freedom!"

"I didn't know that morning that I was going to…make the decision to go to jail," Wash said. "It was part festival, part day of liberation."

So many children wanted to be in on the action, they cheerfully stood in lines a block long, waiting for the big yellow school bus to take them to jail. Within ninety minutes, a thousand jubilant protesters were on their way—almost as many as had been arrested during the previous four days. Most of them were girls. On board the buses, they chanted freedom songs, stomped their feet, and shook their fingers out the windows at police.

"First they took us to City Jail," Wash said. "It was so crowded, they put us outside. There were two guards, who had to

Jailed students, 1963

figure out what the heck to do with all these nappy-headed children—maybe five hundred kids. We were saying, 'We're just as good as you.' A policeman was sitting on a fire escape, and he was listening to us." Wash had never had a conversation with a policeman.

After an hour or two, he and the other kids were bused from City Jail to Juvenile Hall. Again, they were placed outdoors, "in the courtyard," Wash said, "between the buildings, like a natural canyon." The police pulled a rope across the area, putting males on one side, females on the other.

"We started singing," Wash said. "We sang and we sang—all the Movement songs, all the gospel songs… And, there was this young sister. She sang 'The Lord's Prayer.' We all bowed and got down on our knees. I remember seeing the white people in the window who worked there, these clerks and all. They were all looking at us. It was a different kind of look. It was one of the most emotional things in my life. Everybody was quiet. She had a beautiful voice. The prayer is a beautiful prayer, and she sang it."

"Forgive us our trespasses, as we forgive those who trespass against us," she sang. "Deliver us from evil."

It was nearly sunset. "Some of… [the clerks]," Wash said, "had tears in their eyes."

The children who were already in jail suddenly got a lot of company. "As the day progressed," Audrey said, "the rooms filled." She was no longer bored. One of the arrestees sent to Juvenile Hall was a friend who was two years older. Finally, Audrey had someone closer to her own age to play with.

From talking with the new inmates, watching television, and overhearing the matrons' conversations, she learned what was going on downtown. "We would get all excited and smile…and whisper, 'Did you hear the news? We filled up all the rooms!' We'd be all proud about the jails filling up."

The dayroom in which Audrey was held became almost as overcrowded as James's cell. It held around two hundred inmates, mostly younger children, but had only sixty-two beds. Elsewhere, seventy-five prisoners squeezed into pens built for eight. A comedian even in lockup, Dick Gregory quipped, "It was wall to wall us."

Arnetta finally got her chance to be arrested again, just like the other Peace Ponies. She had joined the throngs marching from the church when a group of police and firemen confronted them. She was rounded up and taken to the station. But, to her deep disappointment, she did not manage to get locked up. "They were bringing in so many children," Arnetta said, "they could not keep them. So we were booked and released."

"YOU CAN'T TREAT PEOPLE THIS WAY"

Between Thursday, May 2, and Monday, May 6, almost 2,500 young people had been arrested. Connor could not squeeze one more body into any cell, but he was determined to corral the new arrestees somewhere. He chose the 4-H barns at Fair Park, the state fairground from which, ironically, Negroes were usually banned, except on one Thursday night a year.

It took six hours to process and transport the hundreds of marchers, who were then housed in the cattle pens and hog pavilions. Many stood in the open with no food, water, or place to sleep. At nightfall, it started to rain. Children stood crying in the cold, wet darkness. Hundreds of parents drove to the park to throw blankets and sandwiches over the high fences but the police kept most of them away. Reporters, too, were barred from the area. One who asked to see the prisoners was told, "If you want to see something, there's a lot of good movies downtown."

Wash had been bused a second time from the courtyard of Juvenile Hall to the Jefferson County Jail. He slept on the concrete floor that night, but at least he had been given a sandwich and was protected from the rain.

Several young inmates already inside the City Jail heard the children crying outside. "We all climbed up and looked out the window," Mary Hamilton, a teenage organizer, said. They saw "a good two hundred children out in the rain, just being drenched...the rain was just coming in torrents." Mary and her cellmates banged on their cell walls, trying to get help for them.

Instead of shepherding the youngsters indoors, Mary said, "A mob of policemen came in and herded us all into these solitary-confinement cells, which were about two [feet] by two. You could take two short steps in both directions. Had nothing in them but a little steel seat... There were twelve to fifteen of us in these cells... We were very uncomfortable." After five hours in what she called a "sweatbox" and another teenage inmate described as "a big steel coffin," they banged on the walls to be released. Mary told the police, "The girls have been in here... without bathroom facilities and without water. You can't treat people this way." The police removed all the girls from the cell except Mary. She spent another two hours in solitary before a policeman allowed her to go to the bathroom. Before he did, he walloped her in the head.

"MAKING HISTORY"

"This is the most inspiring movement that has ever taken place in the United States of America," King said at one of the four mass meetings he spoke to that evening. As many as ten thousand people attended the meetings. After the Birmingham Movement Choir performed "I'm On My Way to Freedom Land" at one of them, King went on to say:

There are those who write history. There are those who make history. There are those who experience history. I don't know how many historians we have in Birmingham tonight. I don't know how many of you would be able to write a history book. But you are certainly making history, and you are experiencing history. [Yes!] And you will make it possible for the historians of the future to write a marvelous chapter. Never in the history of this nation have so many people been arrested for the cause of freedom and human dignity. [Yes! That's right!]... Don't worry about your children. [Yeah!]... Don't hold them back if they want to go to jail. [Right!] For they are doing a job for not only themselves but for all of America and for all of mankind." [Yes! Yes!]

Elsewhere, negotiators were deadlocked. Burke Marshall pleaded with the Biracial Subcommittee for hours, pacing the floor the entire time. Nevertheless, the white business leaders refused to desegregate, and Movement leaders refused to call off the marches without agreement on the Points for Progress. In an article entitled "U.S. working to head off a bloodbath," the *Birmingham News* reported, "There is an alarming vacuum of leadership between the two extremes."

Since the beginning of Project C, less than five weeks earlier, a reported 2,425 people, almost all of them students, had been arrested. The jails and fairground were filled to bursting. Downtown businesses were empty. The whole world was watching.

CHAPTER TWELVE

Birmingham police officers take students' signs, 1963

Signs read: "CAN A MAN LOVE GOD and HATE HIS BROTHER"

MAY 7-10, 1963

"NOTHING WAS SAID...ABOUT THE CHILDREN."

TUESDAY, MAY 7

OPERATION CONFUSION

ORGANIZERS DUBBED TUESDAY "Operation Confusion." Their goal was to shut down central Birmingham.

Early that morning, youth leaders routed students from their homes and schools and dispatched them to Sixteenth Street Baptist Church. Fewer than 14,000 black students—out of 34,000 enrolled in Birmingham city schools—were present for roll call. Many of those who had checked in had then checked out, bringing the absentee rate to well over 20,000. At the seven black high schools, 6,300 students skipped. The *Birmingham News* reported that teachers were "holding classes as best they could."

The stakes were high. Superintendent Wright threatened, "[T]hose over sixteen found guilty of participation [will] be expelled from school." Furthermore, parents whose children had unexcused absences were subject to fines of up to $100 and ninety days of hard labor.

Nevertheless, at ten o'clock in the morning, King held a press conference at which he stated that recent events "mark[ed] the nonviolent movement coming of age" and were "the fulfillment of a dream."

Like multiple bursts of firecrackers on the Fourth of July, Operation Confusion was launched at noon. First, a group of fourteen youngsters, some carrying lunch bags and one with a suitcase, emerged in pairs from the church and circled Kelly Ingram Park. When they slipped back into the church, another group sprang out, like a relay team. At the same time, around six hundred black youths converged on the white downtown. They picked up protest signs from "Movement moms" like Mrs. Robey, who were strategically deployed around the area, and headed to eight different stores. Some created confusion by approaching lunch counters, threatening to sit-in, and then leaving. Others touched the stores' merchandise, outraging white sales clerks.

James's mother drove him back downtown. When he saw friends demonstrating, he jumped out of the car. "There he goes," his mother said. James recalled, "They were having fun. They had a big crowd. A policeman pulled up on a motorcycle. As soon as he said, 'You're all under arrest,' everybody scattered in as many different ways as we were individuals. He couldn't do anything about it."

Arrests were no longer an option for the police because city, county, and even surrounding counties' jails were full. Juvenile authorities began calling parents and asking them to come pick up their children; a judge waived the bail bond for many. Wash described the reaction, saying, "It was like, 'If you come get 'em, we'll give 'em to you'... They had to buy new pots, new cooking utensils... It would kill your budget."

Police could do nothing but confiscate and crumple picketers' signs. Blacks called May 7 "Jubilee Day." As Dick Gregory later explained, "Once you arrest three thousand people, you have no control, especially when they ain't scared of you."

After an hour, the young people creating mayhem around town marched to Sixteenth Street Baptist Church where they were greeted by 1,400 compatriots. Along the way, they sang "We Shall Overcome."

Shuttlesworth praised his troops. "Bull Connor thought the jails were like hell to us, but you all have made a heaven out of the jail... You are as good a soldier as any that go across the water. Because you are fighting for what your country is and what it will be."

Hearing raucous cheers from two thousand high-spirited young people in the church and fearing another wave of protests, a policeman asked a Movement leader to encourage them to leave. That idea backfired. The students obliged the policeman by pouring into the park and then swarming back toward the white downtown. Their numbers were doubled when about two thousand spectators joined the stampede. Many chanted, "We're going to ja-il! We're going to ja-il!" Only a couple of dozen could be accommodated that day. The rest satisfied themselves by roaming the streets, celebrating.

King exalted that there were "Negroes on the sidewalks, in the streets…in the aisles of downtown stores. There were square blocks of Negroes, a veritable sea of black faces." Traffic was blocked. White workers out for lunch retreated to their offices. White shoppers fled. Downtown was at a standstill. For blacks, the scene was a dream fulfilled. For storeowners, police, and city leaders, it was a nightmare, especially when, at 2:45 p.m., the mood abruptly shifted.

"HEY, LET'S PUT SOME WATER ON THE REVEREND"

Some in the crowd started hurling rocks and bricks at the police. Officers from five surrounding towns, an armed contingent from a neighboring county, and state troopers all joined Connor's force and retaliated against the mob by chasing and clubbing anyone with dark skin. Black and white pedestrians got into fistfights. Connor lurched up in his armored car. Through loudspeakers, he bellowed commands for the roving youngsters to disperse. When they didn't obey, he called, yet again, for hoses and dogs. The dogs were held in check this time but both observers and protesters were blasted with hoses. At least one of them didn't mind; organizer Andrew Marrisett said, "When they put on the water hose, I took a washcloth, and I bathed."

Shuttlesworth and A. D. King did mind, though. As Bevel had done on Saturday, King borrowed a policeman's bullhorn and tried to squelch the escalating violence. "You're not helping our cause," he called to the rock throwers. "You mustn't taunt the police."

Waving a white handkerchief, Shuttlesworth led about three hundred kids toward Sixteenth Street Baptist Church. A fireman paid no attention to the minister's peace sign and called out, "Hey, let's put some water on the Reverend!" The force of the water rolled Shuttlesworth down the church steps and slammed him into a brick wall. He prayed, "Lord, I've been coming this way a long time. This is it. I'm ready when you are." An ambulance took him to Holy Family Hospital to treat his injuries. Connor said he was sorry he'd missed it and wished the Reverend had been carried away in a hearse.

119

Water hoses and billy clubs finally dispersed the rioters and protesters late that afternoon. But Police Captain Evans knew that brute force would not resolve racial problems in Birmingham. "What does this accomplish?" he wondered. "What do we hope to do here by doing these kinds of things?"

"WE WANT EVERYBODY IN THE STRUGGLE FOR HUMAN DIGNITY"

Mass meetings filled three churches that night, including a students-only meeting at St. Paul's. At Sixteenth Street Baptist, Reverend Ed Gardner addressed frantic families. "We want everybody in this struggle for human dignity," he said. "Perhaps some mothers don't want freedom but our children want freedom... I want all the grandmothers to get this: Stand back."

Bevel fired up students, telling them to forget school the next day. "We want all of the students to be out tomorrow... We intend to have the fire department pumping water. Wear your swimsuit if you want to."

King concluded the mass meeting by describing an evening he'd recently spent with President and Mrs. Kennedy at the White House. "After dinner...they showed me the room where Abraham Lincoln... signed the Emancipation Proclamation. I told him, 'Mr. President, I would like to see you come back in the same room and sign the Second Emancipation Proclamation.'"

TUESDAY, MAY 7– WEDNESDAY, MAY 8

NEGOTIATORS PULL AN ALL-NIGHTER

While central Birmingham dissolved into mayhem outside, Marshall met with the Senior Citizens Committee at the chamber of commerce to discuss black leaders' demands. He conferred with the blacks by telephone. Most members of the committee had no intention of caving in to the "outside agitators" they blamed for the protests. One member wanted the governor to declare martial law to suppress the riots.

Melvin Bailey, the county sheriff, told them that the sole place left to house prisoners was the University of Alabama's football field. He also expressed his fear that, sooner or later, someone was going to get killed. Many committee members worried that if they ringed it with barbed wire, their beloved Legion Field would look like a concentration camp on the nightly national news. Pointing at the chaos outside, Sidney Smyer stated, "If we're going to have a good business in Birmingham, we better change our way of living." By the end of the afternoon, a majority of the committee had grudgingly acknowledged that they were going to have to compromise with King. They didn't agree on any particular compromise, just on the idea of needing to do so. The Biracial Subcommittee was charged with working out the details.

The "responsible Negroes" who were on the subcommittee included Shores, and, from SCLC, King, Abernathy, and Young. Smyer and unidentified leading businessmen constituted the white membership; a representative of Mayor Boutwell's office attended as an observer. Marshall worked back and forth between the two sides.

The subcommittee met throughout the night—first in an office building, then at the mansion of John Drew, a wealthy black insurance executive. As talks continued, many details fell off the agenda. Blacks started by demanding that the settlement address all four of the Points for Progress. By three o'clock in the morning, when they finally reached a tense arrangement, the black representatives had retreated. They offered to call off the demonstrations if the businessmen would agree, in principle, to just two aspects of partial integration: (1) some desegregation of some facilities in some downtown department stores and (2) "'token' employment of Negroes."

A key point left undecided was what to do about all the kids in jail. Could they return to school? Would the city drop charges against them? Would the bail for all of them be dismissed? If not, the Movement would somehow have to scrounge about $250,000 to secure their release.

"AIN'T NO USE SCALDING THE HOG ON ONE SIDE"

Hearing rumors of secret, late-night meetings, Shuttlesworth checked himself out of the hospital on Wednesday morning and—still woozy and wearing his hospital ID—made his way to the Drews, where King, Young, Abernathy, and other black leaders had talked through the night. There, Shuttlesworth learned about the compromises the Biracial Subcommittee had made. He was livid. In his absence, Shuttlesworth believed, King had allowed the Points for Progress to be worn down to a worthless nub. On top of that, King had called off the marches!

"We're not calling anything off," Shuttlesworth insisted. He reminded King of his failure two years earlier in Albany, Georgia—the debacle that had nearly undermined the civil rights movement. "People have said this of you before—that you come in and get people started, and then you go off and leave them to their trouble." He stood to stomp out, but dizzy from medication and weak from his injuries, he sank into a chair.

Abernathy tried but failed to calm Shuttlesworth, who insisted, "with what little strength I have left, I'm gon' get up and lead those three or four thousand kids back in the streets." Over a thousand were already waiting at Sixteenth Street Baptist Church for his go-ahead.

Marshall then confessed that he'd promised President Kennedy he could hold a press conference that afternoon announcing an agreement. Shuttlesworth still refused to compromise. "Ain't no use scalding the hog on one side," he argued. "While the water is hot, scald him on both sides and get him clean. If the water gets cold, you ain't never gon' clean off that hog." (Some people at the gathering recall that Shuttlesworth invoked a different animal: "A snake half dead is as bad as a snake all alive—it'll still bite you.")

"We got to have unity," King pleaded. "We just got to have unity." He finally persuaded the quarrelsome group to come to an accord. Instead of permanently canceling the marches, they agreed on a twenty-four-hour moratorium. If the white power structure refused to sign a written agreement within that time, marches would resume. King and Smyer endorsed the truce at separate press conferences that afternoon.

Despite black leaders' goodwill offer to suspend marches, the city's white leadership quickly revealed its bad faith. An hour after the press conference, Connor rearrested King and Abernathy for having marched without a permit on Good Friday, over three weeks earlier. Judge Brown (the same judge who had disrespected Arthur Shores at James's court hearing) gave the ministers a choice between 180 days in jail or paying a ruinously high bail bond. Fortunately, A. G. Gaston posted the bonds.

The two ministers, along with Shuttlesworth, announced, "We held off on massive demonstrations today as a demonstration of good faith to give the negotiators a chance to work in a calm atmosphere." But, they continued, if the settlement—including dismissing charges against the young people in jail—was not worked out by 11:00 a.m. the next day, protests would proceed.

WEDNESDAY, MAY 8

AUDREY

That same afternoon, another judge released more than five hundred children from jail, no bail required. Audrey was one of them. Mrs. Hendricks had been calling someone she knew at the jail each day to check on her daughter, so she knew when to pick Audrey up. Five older freed students held a press conference at which they testified about the brutal treatment they had suffered in jail. Audrey didn't meet the press, nor did she march again. But she kept attending mass meetings.

"WE ARE GOING TO BE FREE"

That night, more than two thousand people jammed Sixth Avenue Baptist Church, despite the nearly ninety-degree heat. "We are back here tonight on our voyage for freedom," Reverend Gardner intoned. "We are going to be free. Sure as I am standing behind this altar, we are going to be free."

Nineteen rabbis from Jewish congregations around the country joined him at the altar. "We came to applaud you," one said. "We came to applaud your courage and dignity in your struggle."

Another rabbi taught the crowd a Hebrew song, *"Hinei Ma Tov U Ma Naim."* He explained what the words meant: "How good and pleasant it is when brothers live together in harmony." Next he asked everyone to put their arm around the person sitting on either side of them and sing it again, swaying together side to side. Connor's spies had to report that they "were sitting between two negroes, and they really gave us the treatment."

Bevel closed the mass meeting by urging the young people to fill Sixteenth Street Baptist Church the next day. "[I]f the committee lies to us, we will be ready to break

DUELING PRESS STATEMENTS

"[T]here is an important moral issue involved of equality for all of our citizens. And until you give it to them you are going to have difficulties as we have had this week in Birmingham."
—President John F. Kennedy

"[T]he President wants us to surrender this state to Martin Luther King and his group of pro-Communists...I wish to commend Bull Connor and his forces..."
—Governor George Wallace

"It's his duty to put down riots and apprehend subversives and not encourage them..."
—Mayor Art Hanes, regarding Attorney General Robert F. Kennedy

"I have made no commitment with reference to any matters being negotiated."
—Mayor Albert Boutwell

loose and strike... We have had 2,200 people in jail, and today there was 6,000 more that was ready to go," he said. "We have declared war on these people... We will sleep in the streets until they know we want freedom."

Rather than on the streets or in prison, Arnetta, James, and Audrey spent Wednesday night safely at home. Wash, the most reluctant foot soldier, spent another night in jail.

SILENCE

Thursday morning, Audrey returned to Center Street Elementary School. No one asked her about her week in jail, and she didn't say anything. "I was just one of the kids, as everybody else was," she said. "It didn't dawn on me that it was a big deal."

Over fifteen thousand other children obeyed Bevel's command to stay away from school on Thursday, in case they needed to resume marching. When whites lashed out at the tentative settlement, it appeared that the youngsters would march yet again.

Although the mayor's office had sent an informal observer to one meeting of the Senior Citizens Committee's Biracial Subcommittee, no elected officials served as members. Business leaders had simply appointed themselves representatives of the people of Birmingham and had taken

authority, where none technically existed, for determining the city's future way of life.

Calling the white members of the Biracial Subcommittee "a bunch of quisling, gutless traitors," outgoing Mayor Hanes insisted that "if they would stand firm, we would run King and that bunch of race agitators out of town." Connor labeled the agreement a "capitulation by certain weak-kneed white people under threat of violence by the rabble-rousing Negro, King." Ironically, given the state's ban on boycotts, he urged, "The white people and other people of this city should not go in these stores. That's the best way I know to beat down integration in Birmingham." One of the white negotiators, whose name had leaked out, received so many threatening phone calls that he had to change his telephone number.

At eleven o'clock, the deadline for the negotiations came. The committee was silent. The deadline passed. Would the students march again?

King cancelled the press conference at which he was supposed to announce either an agreement on the Points for Progress—including dismissal of charges against the children—or the resumption of marches. Negotiators worked throughout the day, with both sides making concessions. In late afternoon, King told the press that they were close enough to a deal that he could extend the moratorium on marching for one more day.

The biggest sticking point was the charges against the arrested children. King had been negotiating with businessmen, not the school superintendent or city officials who would have the final say in the matter. "The only thing that we can ask of the merchants," he said, "is that they recommend in a very strong manner that the charges be dropped." The merchants, however, had little incentive to make such a recommendation; they were already so terrified of retribution for their role in the negotiations, they refused to be publicly identified. And, even if they made a recommendation, the officials had no reason to act on it.

At the mass meeting that evening, Reverend Abraham Woods announced that national labor unions had raised enough money to bail the remaining 1,500 kids out of jail. But the money was not yet in hand. Banks would be closed over the upcoming weekend, and the children remained incarcerated. Abernathy assured the crowd that if negotiations weren't completed before daybreak, they would return "with their marching shoes on."

Later that night, the Biracial Subcommittee finally reached an agreement. But no one wanted to stand up in public and read it out loud.

THURSDAY, MAY 9

"BIRMINGHAM HAS REACHED AN ACCORD WITH ITS CONSCIENCE"

Blacks and whites had signed off on the agreement together, but each group announced it separately. At 2:30 Friday afternoon, King, Shuttlesworth, and Abernathy gathered at a metal picnic table in the courtyard of the Gaston Motel. Journalists and photographers crowded around them. Shuttlesworth began.

125

Bull Connor reads the press release announcing the agreement to end racial strife in Birmingham, 1963

"The City of Birmingham has reached an accord with its conscience…," he said. "Birmingham may well offer for Twentieth Century America an example of progressive racial relations; and for all mankind a dawn of a new day, a promise for all men, a day of opportunity, and a new sense of freedom for all America…"

He then read the points on which black leaders and white businessmen had agreed.

THE BIRACIAL AGREEMENT

1. The desegregation of lunch counters, rest rooms, fitting rooms and drinking fountains in planned stages within the next 90 days…

2. The upgrading and hiring of Negroes on a nondiscriminatory basis… This will include the hiring of Negroes as clerks and salesmen within the next 60 days…

3. Our movement has made arrangements for the release of all persons on bond or their personal recognizance. Our legal department is working with further solutions in this problem.

4. Through the Senior Citizens Committee or the Chamber of Commerce, communications between Negro and white will be publicly re-established within the next two weeks. We would hope that this channel of communications between the white and Negro communities will prevent the necessity of further protest demonstrations such as have been conducted.

FRIDAY, MAY 10

COMPROMISES ALL AROUND

Compared with the original Points for Progress, the agreement was definitely a compromise. None of the stipulations took effect immediately, as the original Points had demanded. There was no reference to either a biracial committee that would deal with future problems or to "specific plans" for hiring Negroes on the police force and reducing obstacles to voter registration. Above all, there was no mention of dropping "all charges" against the demonstrators. Furthermore, execution of the plan depended on the good will of the merchants, enforcement by city officials, and the cooperation of white citizens—none of which was likely.

King issued a statement. "…[W]e have come today to the climax of a long struggle for justice, freedom and human dignity in the City of Birmingham. I say the climax, and not the end, for though we have come a long way, there is still a strenuous task before us and some of it is yet uncharted."

Nevertheless, King recognized the significance of the achievement. "[I]t is a victory that cannot possibly be confined to the limited area of one race… We must not see the present development as a victory for the Negro: it is rather a victory for democracy and the whole citizenry of Birmingham—

white and black." He added, "[U]ltimate credit and glory and honor must be given to Almighty God, for He has clearly been at work among us." He concluded, "We must now move from protest to reconciliation."

When Shuttlesworth stood to leave the press conference, he fainted.

At another hotel on the white side of town, Smyer announced the agreement on behalf of the Senior Citizens Committee, whose other members, still a mystery, were afraid to appear in public. Smyer felt he needed to explain why the white businessmen had acquiesced to black activists' demands.

"It is important that the public understand," he said, "the steps we have taken were necessary to avoid a dangerous and imminent explosion." He urged Birminghamians to abide by the agreement. "[N]ow that peace has returned to our community, it is up to all to help preserve it by doing nothing which would destroy it."

THE CHILDREN

On Friday, city and county jails released hundreds of children, including Wash. As he and his mother left, he saw matrons bringing huge, new pots and pans to pre-pare food for those left behind. His mother, he says, "didn't whip me, didn't scold me, which let me know that what I had done was alright."

Although none of them felt heroic, Audrey, James, Arnetta, and Wash were jubilant about what they, as four young people in a mass of thousands, had accomplished. White leadership had finally agreed to the principle of integration.

When representatives of the Alabama Christian Movement for Human Rights met with those from the Southern Christian Leadership Conference on Friday, May 10, to discuss the agreement, a member pointed out, "Nothing was said in either statement about the children." Abernathy assured the group that "charges against the students would be dropped. There would be no expulsions or suspensions. This was a definite condition of the cessation of demonstrations."

Ten days later, James learned that, if such a condition had been agreed to, it had been written in disappearing ink.

CHAPTER THIRTEEN

PLAYHOUSE

Armed members of the Alabama Highway Patrol near Sixteenth Street Baptist Church, 1963

MAY 11–MAY 23, 1963

IT WAS THE WORST OF TIMES.
IT WAS THE BEST OF TIMES.

SATURDAY, MAY 11–SUNDAY, MAY 12

"THE KLAN IS RIDING AGAIN"

AT LAST, THERE WAS AN AGREEMENT. But not everyone was in agreement, as all of Birmingham, black and white, learned over the weekend. Hostility to desegregation put nonviolence to the test, and—for a while—nonviolence failed.

On Saturday afternoon, Bevel held a youth rally at Sixteenth Street Baptist Church. Before discussing plans for a voter registration drive, he read aloud from a flier he had come across that morning announcing a Ku Klux Klan rally to be held at 7:30 that night. "White Citizens, Know Your Rights," he read, "The city of Birmingham and the entire United States of America, which was created by your ancestors for your personal benefit, is under attack by Jews and Negro Communist citizens!... Mongrelizers, beware! The Klan is riding again."

Several thousand Klansmen and their families flocked from a half dozen states around the South to a park on the outskirts of Birmingham. Local policemen in uniform also attended.

With the grounds illuminated by two twenty-foot-high flaming crosses, the leader of the Klan, Imperial Wizard Robert Shelton, warned the crowd to resist "demands from any of the atheist so-called ministers of the nigger race…" Ominously, he added, "Martin Luther King's epitaph, in my opinion, can be written here in Birmingham."

Shortly after 8:00 p.m., the switchboard operator at the Gaston Motel answered the phone. The caller told her the Klan was holding a rally just outside of town and asked if King was staying in Room 30, his usual room when he was in Birmingham. Five minutes later, the phone rang again. Another caller asked her if she had a casket for King. The operator reported the threatening calls to Sheriff Bailey, who dismissed her concerns, saying, "If you see anything, call us."

At 10:45, half an hour after the Klan rally ended, a uniformed policeman got out of a squad car and placed a package by the front steps of A. D. King's parsonage. As he drove off, the policeman tossed a second object toward the house. It immediately exploded, creating a small sinkhole in the sidewalk. Hearing the noise, a crowd gathered. Ten minutes later, the original package also exploded, even more powerfully. It was a one-two punch: the first explosion was designed to draw onlookers, the second to injure them, as well as A. D. King and his family.

Bricks shot off the front of the house into the crowd. The front door blew into the kitchen at the back of the house. The living room was suddenly open to the street. Nearly every window was shattered. The roof was propelled forward and hung precariously over the front sidewalk. Amazingly, the entire family escaped unharmed, including Mrs. King, who had been sitting in the living room.

More than a thousand furious bystanders gathered. As police arrived, the crowd flung bricks at them and slashed their tires. Even though his house had just been ruined and he and his family nearly murdered, A. D. King again made the case for nonviolence. Grabbing a bullhorn, as he had the previous Tuesday, he begged the crowd, "Please put your bricks down!"

Just before midnight, a third explosion hit, this one so loud that A. D. King thought his church, only a few blocks away, had blown up. "That's the motel," a Movement leader said, referring to the Gaston Motel, over five miles away.

This bomb, hurled from a speeding Chevrolet, had hit the room directly beneath Room 30. Movement strategists had been meeting in Room 30 for thirty-eight straight days until that Saturday night. The explosion blasted a hole the size of two refrigerators through the steel-reinforced concrete wall, shattered windows in the neighbor-

hood, and destroyed three nearby trailers. Diners and waitresses fled the motel restaurant, screaming. Fortunately, no one was badly hurt.

Though the switchboard operator had informed police of the threatening phone calls, officers had stopped patrolling nearby streets several hours earlier. However, an official police vehicle—assigned to an officer who was the nephew of "Dynamite Bob" Chambliss—accompanied the Chevrolet from the scene.

Despite evidence that the police were involved in both the Klan rally and the bombings that followed, outgoing Mayor Hanes suggested that Martin Luther King Jr. and his fellow civil rights activists were responsible for the explosions.

Even before the details of police involvement were known, blacks retaliated with unleashed frustration and fury. Enraged patrons of nearby pool halls and bars poured into the motel's parking lot, surrounding streets, and Kelly Ingram Park. They threw bottles and chunks of concrete at officers.

Yet again, Movement leaders pleaded with the crowd to disperse. Wyatt Tee Walker tied a white cloth around his arm, climbed on top of a car, and shouted through a bullhorn, "Please do not throw any bricks anymore. Ladies and gentlemen, will you cooperate by going to your homes." A bottle-tosser responded, "How come we have to go home every time *they* start violence?" Someone threw a brick; it slammed into Walker's ankle.

Soon, more than 2,500 people surged into the black downtown. Most, like Wash, wanted to get even. "We threw rocks at white folks' cars," Wash said, "roamed the streets, vandalize, burn anything the white folks owned."

Others went out of curiosity. "I was at home," Arnetta said, "but we got in the car and we came downtown. It was scary—a full riot." After seeing Connor's armored car, the Streeters left and drove over to Ensley to view the damage to A. D. King's house.

Mr. and Mrs. Hendricks also brought Audrey and her sister downtown. As they got close to the motel, though, they saw fires and turned around. "It was a dangerous situation," Mrs. Hendricks said. "We got out of there."

James and his family didn't go downtown that night, but he knew about the bombings and what they meant. "The battle had intensified," he said. "We went to jail... and we won—like a soccer game... The bombings were at a different level; they were trying to kill somebody."

Marauders smashed car windows and looted stores—some owned by whites and others by blacks. Someone stabbed a policeman three times in the back. Rioters pulled a white taxi driver out of his vehicle and stabbed him, then overturned the cab and torched it. When sparks set nearby buildings aflame, the mob prevented fire trucks driven by whites from reaching the site. Police sprayed tear gas from a tank, but the mob refused to disperse. A city block of apartment houses and businesses blazed.

At about 1:30 in the morning, A. D. King, who had finally quelled the mob outside his shattered home, drove to Kelly Ingram Park. Through a megaphone, he called out, "Now if we who were in jeopardy of being killed, if we have gone away *not* angry, *not* throwing bricks...why must you rise up to hurt our cause? You are *hurting* us! You are *not* helping!"

He managed to gather three hundred protesters and lead them in prayer. "Oh, God, we pray that thou would'st give us at this hour the spirit of patience. Give us the spirit of love. Give us the spirit of understanding. And bless our lives and bless this city." Some people sang "We Shall Overcome." Working together, the ministers and some policemen began to convince the crowd to disband and head toward home. A local black civil defense unit also acted heroically; one of its members, James Lay, rescued the white cabdriver, and another member managed to quell one of the fires. By 2:30 in the morning, the riots were nearly spent.

"YOU'RE DAMN RIGHT IT'LL KILL SOMEBODY"

Nevertheless, six hundred state troopers, armed with submachine guns, sawed-off shotguns, and tear gas, rushed to Kelly Ingram Park. They were led by Colonel Al Lingo, the state's director of public safety, and were accompanied by a posse of armed white militants, who were under no one's command. Some rode in on horseback like a cavalry.

Fearing—accurately, it turned out—that the troopers would make things worse, Chief Moore urged Lingo to withdraw. "We don't need any guns down here," he argued. "You all might get somebody killed."

"You're damn right it'll kill somebody," Lingo retorted. He fired off his automatic shotgun and led the troops on a charge down the streets. The *New York Times* reported that blacks "fled in terror as they were clubbed with gun butts and nightsticks. The 'thonk' of clubs striking heads could be heard across the street." Troopers followed Wyatt Tee Walker as he dashed into the Gaston Motel to protect his wife. They knocked her on the head and later beat him, breaking his wrist.

Lingo's beat-'em-up and scare-'em-off tactics not only didn't work any more, they badly backfired. Tensions flared yet again and blacks swept through the area, burning and slashing for another three hours.

As the heat from the fires finally became intolerable and dawn began to dispel the menacing darkness, the riots petered out for a second—and final—time that night. Fifty people, some seriously wounded, had been taken to the hospital. Downtown Birmingham was in shambles; two apartment buildings and seven stores in a nine-block area lay devastated. The editor of the *Birmingham News* called Sunday, May 12, "a sabbath of sorrow." The day was also the second anniversary of the beating of Freedom Riders at the Birmingham Trailways Bus Station.

WHAT ABOUT THE AGREEMENT?

The violence raised an agonizing question: would the agreement hold?

President Kennedy stated his commitment to the agreement on national television that night, saying, "The Birmingham agreement was and is a fair and just accord." But, just in case, he ordered three thousand federal troops to army bases near Birmingham and nationalized the Alabama National Guard, readying them to intervene if violence reignited.

State officials, on the other hand, opposed the compromise. Lingo said, "There wasn't any agreement that I know of." Governor Wallace labeled the Biracial Subcommittee "a group of appeasers who...have played right into the hands of Martin Luther King and his cohorts."

Despite this opposition, Smyer confirmed that the Senior Citizens Committee members would uphold their end of the agreement. King, who returned to Birmingham immediately upon hearing about the riots, concurred. "I do not feel the events," he said, "nullified the agreement at all."

At the mass meeting Sunday evening at New Pilgrim Baptist, King cautioned the flock: "We must work passionately and unrelentingly for first-class citizenship, but we must not use second-class methods to gain it." His brother, A. D., stood next to him as proof. "When the Lord is with you," he said, "even bombs can't hurt you."

Over that weekend, demonstrations were held in dozens of cities to support civil rights in Birmingham. In Washington, DC, three thousand people picketed the Department of Justice. An equal number massed on the Boston Common. Marchers in San Francisco carried placards reading, "Brotherly Love for ALL, not 'Whites Only.'" About one hundred demonstrators protested at the United Nations in New York City. In Philadelphia, 5,000 black church members and 150 ministers rallied at Independence Hall. Reverend Leon Sullivan of Zion Baptist Church called for all religious groups to

join a "holy crusade against intolerance and racial injustice." He concluded, "brotherhood is more than a Sunday word."

MONDAY, MAY 13

"LET NOBODY PULL US SO LOW"

Audrey, Arnetta, and James went to school on Monday. Miss Woolfolk announced to the class that Arnetta had been arrested. "She gave me a big hug," Arnetta said, "made me feel real proud."

Martin Luther King Jr. and Ralph Abernathy visited the same bars and pool halls that the rioters had spilled out of on Saturday night. After playing—and losing—a game of pool, King would gather players around the bar or pool table. As if he were preaching at a mass meeting, he told a group:

I can well understand how we are often driven to the brink of bitterness, and even despair, because of the way we are treated by policemen and highway patrolmen, and the way we are bombed, and our children are exploited…but…it is possible to stand up against all of these evils and injustices without fighting back with violence… [N]ot only is violence immoral in our struggle, but it is also impractical…We make a much greater moral impact when we are the recipients of violence rather than the inflictors…Let nobody pull us so low as to make us hate them…

Then, while drinkers and pool players held hands and sang "We Shall Overcome," King passed around a hat and collected their weapons. Starstruck, some of the men followed him from site to site, until carbine-carrying state troopers blocked King's route and made him return to the damaged Gaston Motel.

Later in the day, Movement leaders received troubling news. On behalf of the Senior Citizens Committee, Smyer announced that the desegregation agreement meant that only "one Negro sales person will be employed in one store." Not, as the civil rights leaders had believed, at least one clerk in *each* store.

Nevertheless, leaders did not call for protests. The mass meeting that afternoon at Sixth Avenue Baptist Church featured two famous athletes who had broken the color barrier in their sports. Floyd Patterson, a former heavyweight-boxing champion, told the crowd how much the achievements in Birmingham meant to blacks in the North. Jackie Robinson, the first black Major League baseball player, said that his children had told him they wanted to march in Birmingham, too. King closed the meeting by emphasizing, "this is not a racial conflict... The tension in Birmingham is between justice and injustice."

Justice was partially served the very next day. Downtown department store owners met the most immediate terms of the agreement by desegregating their dressing rooms.

No one was ready to celebrate, however. Over the next week, Lingo's state troopers remained in Birmingham. To help suppress more conflicts, nearly 17,800 nationalized combat troops patrolled downtown while military helicopters flew noisily overhead. Meanwhile, black and white negotiators bickered over the number of black salespeople the white storeowners were willing to hire.

MONDAY, MAY 20

"YOU ARE EXPELLED"

During roll call on Monday morning, James's homeroom teacher called his name, as usual. But she didn't call the names of everyone in the class. Why was she reading only some names?

"We're looking at each other," James said, "wondering what's the nature of this list... About three-quarters of the way through the people she was calling, we realized they were people we knew who had participated... She got very upset. She got tearful... She said, 'You have to leave the class. You are expelled.' We had to do it. All the people who were expelled had to get up and leave. We were just shocked."

This selective roll call happened at the other black high schools in town, too. The Birmingham Board of Education expelled

1,081 students that day. Juniors, like James, would have to repeat the school year. Seniors would be unable to graduate, ever. King called the expulsion "a tragic move and an immoral move."

Despite her participation, Arnetta was not expelled, but she and other students stayed home from school anyway in the days that followed. "The parents had gotten very, very afraid by this time, and they were holding onto their kids because they were frightened at the things that could happen," she said. "Bull Connor was striking back in whatever way he could."

At the mass meeting that afternoon, Bevel, without consulting other Movement strategists, called for all black students to walk out of their schools in protest. He also distributed thousands of fliers on which, without approval, he had added King's name alongside his.

King had left town over the weekend, but he dashed back to Birmingham. He was worried about how blacks would react to the expulsions. If they rioted again, the desegregation agreement would certainly come undone. He urged the leaders of ACMHR to respond "with restraint and with united calmness," and they cancelled the students' mass meeting that Bevel had scheduled for the next morning. They also arranged for two black attorneys to sue the board of education. Arthur Shores (who had represented James) and Constance Baker Motley, an outside lawyer, sued on behalf of Linda Cal Woods, Reverend Calvin Woods's daughter, for the right of all expelled students to return to school.

In the courtyard of the Gaston Motel, King gathered a group of students who had not been expelled and directed them to return to school on Tuesday. Reluctantly, they acquiesced. He instructed those, like James, who couldn't go back, to "stay home and study."

STUDENTS

WHICH SIDE ARE YOU ON?

The Board of Education has given an order to expel and suspend all students who participated and were arrested during the demonstration to end segregation in Birmingham.

Our motto must remain the same:

"All stay out until all can get in."
"All for one and one for all."
"Which side are you on?"

All students who were expelled or suspended and all students who know those students were right, please answer roll call at the Sixteenth Street Baptist Church at 9 o'clock on Tuesday, May 21, 1963.

FIRST CLASS OF FREEDOM:
Dr. M. L. King, Jr.,
Rev. James Bevel and
Rev. C. Billups

WEDNESDAY, MAY 22

"VICTORY NIGHT"

Despite King's instructions, James said that he and other expelled classmates "spent the next couple of days just walking around... talking about what had happened, what does it all mean, what is going to happen to us... How do I get to college?" On Tuesday, May 21, students met with King and asked to send representatives to ACMHR meetings to help plan a response to the board of education.

On Wednesday evening, May 22, James and his friends decided at the last minute to go to the mass meeting at New Pilgrim Baptist. "We almost didn't go," he said, "and we went in late, and we sat on the last row in the back... Constance Motley said, 'We are going to give these American flags to each one of you... We will start in the back and you just come down and get the flags.'" James was the first one to receive a flag, just as he had been the first person out the door of Sixteenth Street Baptist Church on May 2.

The speakers described what had happened: the federal judge in Birmingham had ruled against Linda Cal Woods. James's heart sank at this news. But then, the speakers continued, Woods's lawyers had quickly appealed the decision to the circuit court in Atlanta. That court had decided that the expelled students could return to school.

"There was a huge roar in the place, and people were excited...," James said. "That restored my faith..." He and 1,500 other young marchers exuberantly waved their flags.

Dr. King announced that the court's decision proved that "the students who engaged in these peaceful protests were not only moving down a path of morality but they were moving within constitutional paths... This vindicates our actions, and it vindicates our movement."

Connor's spies reported, "Tonight was their victory night."

THURSDAY, MAY 23

"WORST DAY"

On Thursday, May 23, 1963, the Alabama Supreme Court unanimously ruled Albert Boutwell the winner of the mayoral election. The city council replaced the commissioners, who cleaned out their offices that afternoon. Bull Connor was out of a job. "This," he said, "is the worst day of my life."

CHAPTER FOURTEEN

Whites taunt black demonstrators during a protest in Gadsden, Alabama, 1963

FREEDOM AND FURY

THE WALLS FALL DOWN.

IN HIS ANNUAL ADDRESS to the ACMHR on June 5, 1963, Shuttlesworth said:

> ...how glorious it is to realize that Negroes in Birmingham, Alabama, have not only helped to bring about a change in local government, but also a change in the attitude of the National government about the racial situation... We are closer to freedom because the Negro in this city united as never before. Both young and old, students and adults, middle class, low class and no class, all joined together to put on the biggest mass demonstration ever to occur in America... Police dogs, the police lines and the water hoses could not put out the fire that started burning in Birmingham.

Shuttlesworth gave his talk the perfect title: "A Little Closer to Freedom." Blacks in Birmingham were closer but, sadly, had not yet reached freedom's land. Audrey, Wash, Arnetta, and James still could not choose which park to play in or which water fountain to drink from.

139

While the events of April and May 1963—especially the children's marches—brought about an agreement between Birmingham's white business leaders and the black population, actually implementing that agreement required many more months (years, even) of efforts that yielded success only in fits and starts.

Most whites still wanted nothing to do with integration. The brand-new city councilmen hadn't participated in the negotiations and felt little responsibility for the results. In an article about the Biracial Subcommittee, the *Birmingham News* wrote, "These white citizens...had no authority. They did *not* speak for *any* elected city officials. They did not speak for *any* citizens... Negroes obviously accepted that...nothing that anyone 'agreed upon' was binding."

The marches were over but the lawsuits, bombs, and riots continued. Reactions to the agreement—and reactions to the reactions—yo-yoed back and forth throughout the summer and into September.

Some hopeful changes occurred almost immediately. On June 5, the Tutwiler, Birmingham's ritziest hotel, voluntarily began accepting black guests. On June 23, downtown department stores removed "White" and "Colored" signs from bathrooms and drinking fountains.

The next week, newly designated Mayor Boutwell desegregated the city's golf courses as his first official action under the agreement. He did not desegregate playgrounds or swimming pools, however, claiming the city did not have the funds. Parks had been more heavily used by blacks than golf courses, and they remained closed into the late 1960s. But it was a baby step in the right direction. Public libraries had been informally desegregated by demonstrators and were soon officially integrated. Their bathrooms, however, were not and remained locked; all patrons—black and white—had to seek facilities elsewhere.

In mid-July, Boutwell appointed the biracial commission called for in the Points for Progress. Of the 212 members, only 27 were black, and none of the black members was given a leadership position.

On July 23, 1963, the city council took the most dramatic step of all: it repealed Birmingham's Segregation Ordinances. Suddenly, it was legal "to conduct a restaurant or other place for the serving of food in the city, at which white and colored people are served in the same room..." The following week, restaurants in downtown department stores and five-and-dimes integrated their restaurants and lunch counters. Within a month, those in suburban shopping centers followed suit.

The repeal of the ordinances also officially applied to taverns, movie theaters, pool and billiard rooms, bowling alleys, railroads and street railroads, toilets, buses, and taxis. But not to public schools or universities.

"I GOT SOME ICE CREAM!"

Arnetta's mother received a phone call from her friend Lucinda Robey. Could Arnetta and her sister Joan test the repeal of segregation by going to the movies and out to lunch? Mrs. Streeter agreed. "The first place we went," Arnetta said, "was to the Alabama Theatre. Mrs. Robey picked us up and provided the money that we needed."

Arnetta, Joan, and two other black girls walked up to the ticket booth and bought tickets. Then, for the first time, they entered the theater through the front door and sat downstairs. "For whatever reason," she says, "I was not scared." The girls didn't stay all the way through the movie; they were just there to test the owners' compliance with the agreement. On the same day, they also bought tickets and went to movies at the Lyric and the Melba Theatres. They had never been inside the Melba before; it didn't have a balcony, which under the Segregation Ordinances was the only place blacks had been allowed to sit.

Later they ate at two restaurants. "They were very polite," Arnetta said about the waitresses at one location, "overly courteous because they realized we were testing. The only problem that we had throughout the day was when we went to a hot-dog stand. They put a lot of hot sauce on the hot dog. We didn't know until we bit down on it."

Adults who tested integration of eating facilities were also, generally, served without incident. Reverend Calvin Woods sent teams to order lunch at formerly all-white restaurants and reported, "The waitresses were very cordial while the cooks looked on with quiet amazement." What a change from April 3, when a white man spat at him as he sat at a lunch counter!

A couple of establishments balked. One waitress ran out of Woolworth's when testers sat down at the counter. And blacks had to sue Ollie's, a barbecue restaurant that refused to integrate until the U.S. Supreme Court ordered the owner to do so, over a year later.

Soon, Wash, too, got what he had wanted more than anything. "I went to Newberry's," he said, "and I got some ice cream." He couldn't afford a banana split but he was able to eat upstairs, not in the basement, at a "diner-style, stainless steel bar with stools and a soda machine with pictures of food on the wall."

Audrey, too, went with her parents to restaurants where they had never been able to eat. Before that, she said, "you could only…look through the window."

James didn't venture immediately into desegregated Birmingham. He and his friends just watched what was happening. "We were happy to see that occur and to know that the walls were down," he said. "I went to the Alabama Theatre after a while and saw a movie while sitting downstairs. Sitting in the appropriate place was a weird feeling."

Some white people were relieved by integration, too. Pam Walbert's mother said, "It gave us a sense of freedom…because we were all victims of the system."

"BIRMINGHAM PUT A SPOTLIGHT ON NATIONAL RACISM"

The results of what came to be known as the Children's March (also the Children's Crusade) resonated throughout the country. "Birmingham put a spotlight on national racism," James pointed out. "Because it was widely televised, and they brought out the dogs and the water hoses, then racism was so exposed. That sparked demonstrations all around the country."

People everywhere clamored for the kinds of changes that Audrey, Wash, Arnetta,

and James had helped bring about in Birmingham. During the late spring and summer, nearly fifteen thousand demonstrators, most of them young people, took part in at least 758 nonviolent protests in 186 cities.

In some towns, novice activists needed guidance from the experienced young picketers and marchers from Birmingham. In July, teens from Birmingham helped organize almost a dozen marches in St. Augustine, Florida. Gwendolyn Sanders and her sisters joined a busload of children to help integrate the city's lunch counters. Sixteen-year-old Gwendolyn was a protesting pro; she had participated in nonviolence training, picketed stores, and persuaded other students to join the Movement. She had been arrested and jailed twice.

When Gwendolyn tried to place an order at an International House of Pancakes in St. Augustine, she was arrested and spent four days in jail. Another week, while she was marching with three hundred people through the town square, whites jumped from behind bushes and beat them. Gwendolyn was hit in the head and spent a week in the hospital. Despite these assaults, she went on to demonstrate in Atlanta, Georgia, and Anniston and Gadsden, Alabama. Actions such as these led to the desegregation of public facilities in at least 261 cities around the country that summer.

"A MORAL ISSUE"

The escalating number and fervor of protests, along with pressure from Movement leaders in Birmingham and elsewhere, at last persuaded President Kennedy that he had to take a stand on civil rights. On June 11, 1963, Governor Wallace attempted to prevent two black students from enrolling at the University of Alabama by standing in the doorway to block their entrance. His grandstanding failed, however, and he was forced to step aside and let them enter. That night, President Kennedy delivered an address on national television.

It ought to be possible...for every American to enjoy the privileges of being American without regard to his race or his color. This is not a sectional issue. Difficulties over segregation and discrimination exist in every city, in every state of the Union, producing in many cities a rising tide of discontent...

We are confronted primarily with a moral issue... The heart of the question is whether all Americans are to be afforded equal rights and equal opportunities... One hundred years of delay have passed since President Lincoln freed the slaves, yet their heirs, their grandsons, are not fully free... And this nation...will not be fully free until all its citizens are free.

• College students in Jackson, Mississippi, held a sit-in for three hours at a Woolworth's lunch counter while young whites poured ketchup, mustard, sugar, and paint on them—and, when the protesters still refused to leave, beat them. Other young people marched toward downtown Jackson, waving flags and singing; when police confronted them, they politely waited in line to be arrested. There were so many, they nearly filled the jails.

• Demonstrators tried every day for a week to integrate two movie theaters in Greensboro, North Carolina. Approximately 1,135 of them, mostly college and high school students, were arrested. Jesse Jackson, who was then a local college student, said, "When a police dog bites us in Birmingham, people of color bleed all over America."

• About one thousand marchers were tear-gassed and two hundred "juveniles" arrested in Savannah, Georgia, filling the jails.

• A total of ninety-seven juveniles, some as young as twelve years old, were arrested after they defied an order not to march in Athens, Georgia.

• A group of 220 black students was arrested for trying to integrate a theater in Tallahassee, Florida.

The events in Birmingham and elsewhere have so increased the cries for equality that no city or state or legislative body can prudently choose to ignore them.

A week later, he submitted to Congress a civil rights bill that focused on voting rights, equal employment, and the desegregation of public accommodations, facilities, and schools. When he met with King and other Movement leaders at the White House several days later, the president acknowledged the impact of Birmingham's children on the nation.

"THAT'S THE GUY WHO SPOKE TO US"

In early August, organizers in Birmingham scheduled Salute to Freedom '63, a concert to raise money for local activists to attend the March on Washington for Jobs and Freedom. Famous musicians such as Sammy Davis Jr., Ray Charles, and Marian Anderson were scheduled to appear. The University of Alabama stadium was the largest public arena, but it still barred black performers. City officials also refused to house the event at Municipal Auditorium. The concert was held at Miles College instead and raised enough money for busloads of people to head to Washington for the August 28 mass march.

James attended an integrated summer camp in Massachusetts in mid-August. At the end of the session, the campers—both black and white—went to Washington for the march. James was excited but the other campers were even more enthusiastic—they had someone from Birmingham traveling with them. They arrived early in the morning, and James went searching for friends from home. After walking past fifty or sixty buses, he found several. They sat and talked together near the Reflecting Pool in front of the Lincoln Memorial. When James turned around, he saw "people all the way back to

March on Washington, 1963

the [Washington] Monument. That was shocking. I didn't have any idea how many people were behind us. There were throngs."

The throngs numbered about 250,000. King called the event "the greatest demonstration for freedom in the history of our nation."

James listened along with the crowd to speeches by religious and civil rights leaders and to musicians. One of the singers, Odetta, was born in Birmingham. At the end of the program, King delivered his "I Have a Dream" speech, parts of which he had rehearsed at a mass meeting at Sixteenth Street Baptist Church the previous April. Applause and calls of "That's right!" and "Amen!" punctuated practically every sentence. James was especially exhilarated. "We knew him," he said. "That's the guy who spoke to us in the churches and the meetings. And, now he's on the national stage."

SCHOOL INTEGRATION? YES AND NO

After the march, James spent a week in Washington with his grandmother before returning to Birmingham to start his senior year at Ullman High. While he was in DC, a judge in Birmingham approved the city's plan to desegregate public schools. In retaliation, someone bombed Arthur Shores's home. In response to that bombing, more than a thousand blacks rioted until A. D. King yet again persuaded them to disperse.

When school started on September 4, Dwight and Floyd Armstrong took the city up on its desegregation plan. (The two brothers had previously tried to register at a white school when Mr. Streeter wanted Arnetta and her sister to do the same.) Though jeered by hundreds of angry white demonstrators, they entered the fifth and sixth grades of Graymont School. Three other black students integrated two high schools.

Later that week, for the second time in ten days, someone bombed the Shores family's home. There was less damage this time, but the ensuing riot was worse. Over twenty people were injured, and one black person was killed by police bullets, which police claimed fell out of the sky after being shot over rioters' heads.

Five days after school started, Governor Wallace signed an executive order stating, "No student shall be permitted to integrate the public schools of the City of Birmingham, Alabama."

THE WALLS OF THE CHURCH

In early September, Carolyn Maull, a friend of James's who had been hosed during the marches, asked him if he was available on

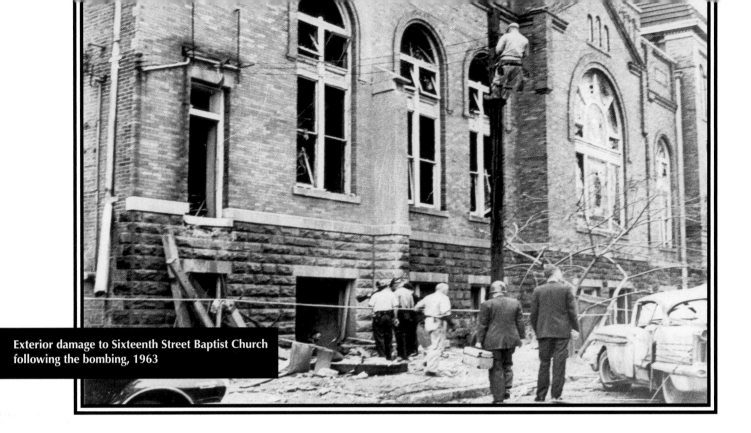

September 15 to teach a Sunday school class at Sixteenth Street Baptist Church. The minister, Reverend John Cross, had designated the date Youth Day, and Carolyn was looking for young people to come to the church and describe their experiences with the Movement. James declined the invitation and stayed home that morning.

Arnetta was at home, too. "It was a dark-looking day," she said. "It should not have been dark because it was so early in the year but it was dark and gloomy."

At about 10:20, the telephone rang in the church office. Carolyn lifted the receiver. "Two minutes," she heard but she didn't understand what the caller meant.

She walked out of the office and up the hall toward the steps that led to the sanctuary, which was filled with a couple of hundred worshippers, nearly half of them youngsters.

Less than two minutes later, ten to fifteen sticks of dynamite exploded.

"One minute, a typical Sunday school day," Mamie Greer, the Sunday school's superintendent said, "the next, window glass and debris flying everywhere, people screaming and practically stampeding to get out."

The blast killed four girls and nearly blinded another, the sister of one of the victims. Twenty other people were injured.

During the previous night, vigilantes

had carefully placed dynamite under the side steps that led to the basement near the ladies' restroom, where the girls were hurriedly primping before service. These were the same steps Arnetta had marched up on May 2, the same steps where Shuttlesworth had been injured by the blast of water on May 7.

Cross picked his way to the front of his shattered church. He didn't yet know that four small girls lay so crushed and mutilated in the basement that they were unrecognizable. Echoing the lesson of the day, "The Love That Forgives," he admonished the furious crowd that gathered, "We should be forgiving, as Christ was forgiving..." Reverend Billups added, "Go home and pray for the men who did this evil deed... We must have love in our hearts for these men."

But their homilies did not persuade everyone to go home and pray. "Anything we could get our hands on owned by white folks, we destroyed it," Wash said, describing the riot that followed the bombing. "We got a big croker sack and just filled it with rocks. These people [a white couple] were in a red and white Impala convertible, and we dropped that whole sack of rocks" off the viaduct. "All we knew is that white folks had bombed the church, and we were going to get even."

Cynthia Wesley. Denise McNair. Carole Robertson. Addie Mae Collins. They were four girls—all of them fourteen years old, except for Denise McNair, who was eleven— four out of tens of thousands of school children. Yet, it seemed that just about every black person in Birmingham felt connected to one or another of them.

Cynthia was in Arnetta's sister's class at Ullman High and belonged to the Cavalettes, the sister group to James's social

147

Window damage to Sixteenth Street Baptist Church following the bombing, 1963

club. Arnetta's mother had graduated from Tuskegee with Denise's father. Denise's mother taught at Center Street Elementary, where both Denise and Audrey went to school. Carole's father taught music at Washington, the elementary school Wash, James, and Arnetta had attended, and the Robertsons were close to the Stewarts. "Two of those girls," James said, "were very close friends."

Carole's funeral was held on September 17. Her mother asked James to help carry the casket. "I stepped up," James said. When one of the other pallbearers nearly dropped the casket, James steadied him. "The funeral was something that I just walked through…," James said. "It was like being numb… It was horrible. Carole was a sweet girl… It was just horrible."

A combined funeral for Cynthia, Denise, and Addie Mae was held on September 18. The service drew six thousand people, both black and white, and was covered by reporters from around the world. King eulogized the children as "heroines of a holy crusade." Arnetta, who attended with the Peace Ponies, said, "There was not a dry eye."

Cynthia, Denise, Carole, and Addie Mae were not the only black children killed in Birmingham on September 15, 1963. Virgil Ware, thirteen, was riding on the handle-bars of his brother's bicycle when he was shot by a sixteen-year-old white Eagle Scout on his way home from an anti-integration rally. The killer, Larry Joe Sims, said he pulled his gun on Virgil because he was afraid the Wares might throw rocks at him. A policeman also shot to death sixteen-year-old Johnnie Robinson, who, like Wash, was throwing rocks at whites' cars.

Six young black people dead in one day.

"To know that somebody hated us as a people," James said, "hated us so much that they decided the way to win is to now kill their children… That was very sobering. It made me angrier, but it made me more determined."

Sobered. Angry. Determined. This is the way many people in Birmingham, the country, and the White House felt in September 1963.

Sobered by racism.

Angry about violence.

Determined to gain civil rights.

"THE POPULARTIY OF HATRED"

The day after the church bombing, a white lawyer named Charles Morgan gave a talk to a club for young white Birmingham businessmen. He told them, "The death of those four little girls was your fault as much as it was the guy who made the bomb… Most of all, blame all who looked the other way. Every person in this community who has in any way contributed...to the popularity of hatred is at least as guilty, or more so, than the demented fool who threw that bomb... We are a mass of intolerance and bigotry." Five weeks later, deluged by death threats after these remarks, Morgan and his family left Birmingham for good.

Three men were ultimately charged in the church bombing, though not until many years later. "Dynamite Bob" Chambliss, who had also bombed Shuttlesworth's home in 1956, was convicted of murder in 1977; Thomas Blanton Jr., in 2001; and Bobby Frank Cherry, in 2002. One of the lead prosecutors in Blanton's and Cherry's cases was a white lawyer who had grown up in Birmingham. He was a child at the time of the church bombing, and, like many young whites, was completely unaware of it at the time.

CIVIL RIGHTS

The tragedy propelled President Kennedy and his successor, President Lyndon B. Johnson, to push relentlessly for the Civil Rights Bill, which became law the following summer. In the years after that, more legislation, court decisions, marches, sit-ins, pickets, and pray-ins were required to seek and increasingly secure equal opportunity for all of America's citizens—opportunities to work, go to school, live, shop, and vote as they please.

The process to establish equal rights for all cost many lives and took longer than everyone had hoped. Yet, beginning on the morning that Audrey Faye Hendricks woke up with freedom on her mind, she, Wash, James, Arnetta, and about four thousand other young blacks freed more people than they could have imagined. They were only four individuals amid thousands, but every one had a job to do.

As one of the youngest marchers, Audrey embodied the fearlessness of a child determined to get what's fair. As a leader who became involved in the Movement early on, Arnetta modeled the ideals of non-violent direct action. As the first protester out the church door, James displayed the risks teens were willing to take to be free. And, as a "bad boy" whose faith emboldened him, Wash acted out of outrage but also with redemption.

In the battle for civil rights, each was a foot soldier. Each is a war hero.

CHAPTER FIFTEEN

NO MORE

Congress of Racial Equality conducts a march in memory of Negro youngsters killed in Birmingham bombings, All Souls Church, Sixteenth Street, Washington, DC; (inset) Audrey Faye Hendricks, age 19

BIRMINGHAMS

AFTERWORLD

THROUGH THE INDIGNITIES they suffered, the risks they took, and the successes they achieved, Audrey, Wash, James, and Arnetta transformed Birmingham and America, as well as themselves. Reverend Abraham Lincoln Woods said that, as a result of the Children's March, "The young people recognized their 'somebody-ness.'" Our four heroes grabbed hold of the rights they secured and continued to grow into Somebodies.

AUDREY

When she graduated from Center Street Elementary, Audrey volunteered to join the first class to integrate Ramsey High School.

"For the first two weeks, we all sat in the auditorium," she said, "because they didn't quite know what to do with us. I wasn't Audrey. I was part of the 'Nigra' children group.

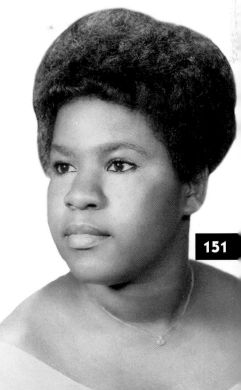

151

Teachers [said], 'Now, you Nigra children, you go over there and sit down.' There were fights; there was resentment. It took a while for whites and blacks to work together. But it was what we fought for."

Audrey's mother also benefited from her daughter's and her own work for the Movement. She was one of the first blacks hired by the federal government in Birmingham. Mrs. Hendricks was elated when managers "warned the white [employees] that…if they participated in any way in opposing integration of the work force, they would be fired."

Audrey attended college and held her first professional job in Dallas, Texas. After eight years there, she was drawn back to

152

Washington Booker III, age 17

Birmingham, where she worked for more than twenty-five years with young children from low-income families. Her sister, Jan, described Audrey as "an advocate for children" and said that her career "gave her a sense of purpose." Schools around the country invited the youngest marcher to talk about her experiences; one presented Audrey with a new board game. In 2007, she earned a master's degree. Her thesis focused on women—like herself, her mother, and Mrs. Robey—who were active in the civil rights movement. Audrey Faye Hendricks, known as the Civil Rights Queen, died in Birmingham in 2009.

WASH

Wash was kicked out of school for the last time during his senior year of high school, shortly before graduation but after his official photograph was taken. He joined the Marine Corps in 1968, and served as a combat soldier in Vietnam, where he once spent four days under artillery fire. A year later, after being recommended twice for a Silver Star and awarded a Bronze Star with Combat-V, he says, he "came back militant." He and his buddies assumed that, while they were fighting, "America had become a fair and a more just place and that black people now shared equally in the American dream." What he discovered when he returned, instead, was "rampant police brutality." Even worse, "I didn't see...unity among black people."

In response, he helped found the Alabama Black Liberation Front, affiliated with the radical Black Panther Party. His organization started breakfast-for-kids programs and followed the police on their patrols to be sure they provided due process to suspects.

"We would get in [our] car and get right behind them," he says. "And if they would stop anybody, we'd get out and...say, 'You have to read him his rights...' They [the police] were really stunned because here was some black men in Birmingham, Alabama, walking up to the police, saying 'This man has a constitutional right to defend himself.'"

Later, Wash earned a high school diploma through the Graduate Equivalency Degree program, joined the Birmingham Fire Department as one of its first black firemen, fought forest fires, directed a traveling theater troupe called the Black Fire Company, and won a state competition to teach poetry for a year in a suburban school district. After teaching, he campaigned for Richard Arrington, who was elected Birmingham's first black mayor in 1979. At campaign headquarters, Wash explained, "I started doing everything from taking out the trash to writing a radio spot...and I ain't been home since."

He remains active in politics, consulting on campaigns and working to be sure eligible voters are registered and go to the polls. He is married and helped raise three children. Although he didn't officially graduate from Ullman High School, his classmates asked him to speak at their thirtieth class reunion.

About the children's marches, Wash says, "It's just a blessing to have been there."

Washington Booker III, 2010

JAMES

At the suggestion of members of the American Friends Service Committee, a Quaker group that helped southern blacks go to college in the North, James attended Case Western

Reserve University in Cleveland, Ohio, after he graduated from Ullman. "I wanted to get as far away from Birmingham as I possibly could," he said. At first, he found the move shocking. He discovered that white students there walked, talked, and danced differently than he was used to. More important, in his first chemistry class, he was expected to use lab equipment that he'd never seen before; Ullman hadn't provided them. "I was an A student," James said about his high school years, "and took advantage of everything that was given to me, and it was all substandard."

As he had at home, James quickly became a leader, cofounding the university's Black Student Union Association. He entered grad-uate school in Detroit, Michigan, but was drafted. After two years in the army, he returned to Birmingham to work as health director for Head Start's Health Services. He also cofounded the statewide Sickle Cell Anemia Project for children with this disease. Later, he worked with the University of Alabama at Birmingham's Project Black Awareness, which recruited and counseled black students to go to college and graduate school. In 1986, James began a career in pharmaceuticals in Atlanta, Georgia, where he lives.

James is married, and he and his wife have four grown children. When he visits Birmingham, he gets together with Wash and Arnetta. He still eats Three Musketeers candy bars and owns the flag he waved on the day he was told he could go back to school.

James Stewart, 2010

James Stewart in college

ARNETTA

After graduating from Ullman High School, Arnetta went to Miles College. She then earned a master's degree in elementary education with an emphasis on mathematics from the University of Alabama at Birmingham. She taught mathematics at white middle schools in the city for several years. Then, even though the classes were larger and the equipment scarcer, she requested a transfer to a predominantly black school.

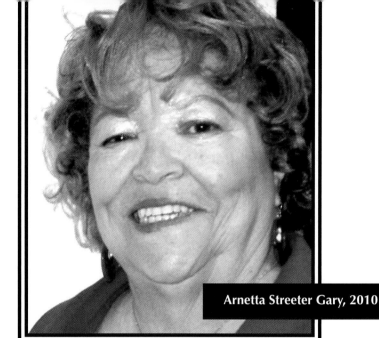

Arnetta Streeter Gary, 2010

Arnetta Streeter, age 19

"I wanted to work with my own children," she says. After thirty-two years, she retired from the Birmingham Public Schools and until 2011, taught mathematics at Miles College. "I feel like being an educator is a blessing the Lord gives you," Arnetta says about her years working with young people. She and her husband, Walter, have one son.

Arnetta also facilitates an after-school program at the Birmingham Civil Rights Institute (BCRI) where she sometimes sees her favorite teacher, Miss Woolfolk. She also remains in touch with one of the other Peace Ponies. Looking back, Arnetta says, "We had no idea the change that was going to come about. It was God's time to make a change."

ONWARD

Participation in the civil rights movement changed the lives of Audrey, Wash, James, and Arnetta, and made them proud of what they achieved. Audrey said, "I see black people walking down the street in their suits and ties, [and I] say, 'Hmm. I had a part in that.'"

Wash knows that "the Movement would have died…had it not been for us… We changed the course of history." He believes that "the most important benefit was the self-esteem it gave black people, the feeling that we can do something."

But Audrey, Wash, James, and Arnetta also have deep concerns. Young blacks today, they said, are not fulfilling the mission the demonstrators aimed for in 1963. Arnetta says that some black children today, "don't realize how far they've come;" she worries that, "they're not taking advantage of it." Their fellow marcher Gwendolyn Sanders fears that high dropout rates and high levels of violence in black communities "abuse all the things that we went to jail for and that Dr. King and so many others lost their lives for." Audrey admitted, "When my own people are not doing well, it grieves my heart. It grieves my heart."

Nevertheless, all agree with James, who said that President Obama "stood on the shoulders of civil rights" to attain his level of education and political office. Blacks in Birmingham have been appointed to the police force and elected to city council and the mayor's office over the years; the city's political structure has become considerably more integrated. Today, Kelly Ingram Park is dedicated to the events that occurred there in 1963, which are depicted in statues scattered around the park.

The Birmingham Civil Rights Institute, a resource and education organization that promotes human rights, sits across the street from the park and Sixteenth Street Baptist Church. At the forty-fifth reunion of the foot soldiers in 2008, a marcher summed up the changes, saying "We've come a long way… We have moved the [segregation] sign off the bus. We have moved from the back of the bus to the front. We are driving the bus."

FORWARD

Audrey, Wash, James, and Arnetta showed that today's problems need not be tomorrow's.

"With commitment, things can change," Audrey said.

Whose commitment?

Children, James said, "are not too young to be involved in what's going on around them. We, as children, got involved in what would appear to be adult issues. One of the primary reasons it worked was that we were children. And God's hand was upon us."

AUTHOR'S NOTE

What happened?

That's the basic question about history, whether an event took place thousands of years or only minutes ago. And it's one of the hardest questions in the world to answer, even when people who saw it happen are still around to tell the story. Sometimes witnesses and participants make it even harder to know!

That's because three people looking at the same event can see it from three different angles. Over time, as their memories shift and opinions harden, they might relate dramatically different accounts of what happened. This process is nearly inevitable, especially when the participants were frightened at the time of the event, as were most of the four thousand or so young marchers who lived in Birmingham during the civil rights movement.

Occasionally, the recollections that Audrey, Wash, James, Arnetta, and others shared with me differed from the written record. In these cases, I asked more questions, read more books and newspapers, studied more maps and photographs. This work was also necessary because many original records of the events were destroyed. History is facts. History is also stories. In merging participants' memories with many other sources, my guidepost was always to tell their stories as truly as possible.

In doing so, I used my judgment but the stories remain theirs not mine.

Why did I choose to tell them? Like Wash, James, and Arnetta (and even more like Charles, Susan, and Pam), I was a teenager in 1963, living in Ohio. Although I read newspaper articles about the marches, hoses, and dogs, it wasn't until I was an adult, writing about music in the civil rights period for *Cobblestone* magazine, that I learned the heart of the story: all of the protesters assaulted and jailed that May were children.

How could I not have known? I had even taught American history to junior-high and high school students! My ignorance embarrassed me.

Many people, I realized, needed to know how a Children's March changed American history. So, I set out to learn what happened.

1944

Birmingham adopts first set of Segregation Ordinances.

1956

JUNE: Reverend Fred Shuttlesworth founds the Alabama Christian Movement for Human Rights (ACMHR). Audrey's mother becomes Corresponding Secretary; the Hendricks family attends weekly meetings.

DECEMBER 20–26: Following desegregation of buses in Montgomery, Alabama, Shuttlesworth demands that Birmingham desegregate buses. Shuttlesworth's home is bombed. He and Audrey's father sit in the front of a bus and are arrested.

1957

SEPTEMBER: When Shuttlesworth tries to enroll his children in a white high school, he is beaten. Arnetta's father tries to persuade her and her sister to enroll in a white school. They refuse.

1959

Audrey's parents sue Birmingham to desegregate public parks.

1961

MAY 14: Freedom Riders are severely beaten in Birmingham. Audrey's father rescues other Freedom Riders in Anniston, Alabama.

OCTOBER: Court desegregates public parks. City Commissioners appeal the decision; they are re-elected to four-year terms.

1961 - 1962

NOVEMBER–JULY: Civil rights campaign in Albany, Georgia, fails. Activists question Dr. Martin Luther King Jr.'s leadership.

1962

JANUARY: Commissioners close public parks.

MARCH: College students begin Selective Buying Campaign.

NOVEMBER: Voters approve change in city government.

1963

JANUARY: King and Shuttlesworth plan to desegregate Birmingham by filling the jails.

APRIL 2: Albert Boutwell elected mayor. Commissioners refuse to leave office. Birmingham has two governments.

APRIL 3: Project C begins. College students organize daily sit-ins, pickets, and marches, which James observes. Audrey's mother asks Bull Connor for permit to march; he refuses.

APRIL 6: ACMHR issues "Points for Progress" and begins holding nightly mass meetings, which Audrey attends. Arnetta hears King's sermon this week and she and Peace Ponies begin training in nonviolence.

APRIL 12: King and others march, defying an injunction, and are jailed. Few other adults are jailed; Reverend James Bevel encourages children to join protests.

APRIL 13: Arnetta participates in her first demonstration.

APRIL 20: King is released from jail. Arnetta pickets and is jailed.

APRIL 22–23: Arnetta is released from jail and testifies at a youth rally.

APRIL 29: Few adults are demonstrating. Jails are not filled. Project C is about to collapse.

APRIL 30: Audrey tells her mother she wants to march.

MAY 2: D-Day. James and Audrey march and are jailed with hundreds of other students

MAY 3: Double D-Day. Arnetta is hosed. Other students are bitten by dogs, and hundreds more are jailed. Wash throws rocks at the police.

MAY 4: Riots break out. President Kennedy sends negotiator to Birmingham.

MAY 5: Miracle Sunday. Firemen refuse to hose marchers. James is released from jail.

MAY 6: Wash marches and is arrested. Jails are filled. James appears in court.

MAY 7: Operation Confusion/Jubilee Day. Protesters fill downtown. Shuttlesworth is hosed. Negotiators work all night.

MAY 8: ACMHR declares a 24-hour moratorium on protests, pending agreements. Audrey is released from jail.

MAY 9: Negotiators fail to reach agreement.

MAY 10: Negotiators announce compromise settlement, desegregating lunch counters and dressing rooms; status of students is unclear. Wash is released from jail.

MAY 11: Ku Klux Klan holds rally. A. D. King's home and Gaston Motel are bombed. Wash joins ensuing riot, which Audrey and Arnetta observe.

MAY 20: James and over 1,000 other students are expelled from school. The Movement sues.

MAY 22: James learns that the students are re-admitted.

MAY 23: Boutwell is declared mayor. Connor is ousted from office.

JUNE 11: President Kennedy gives speech on civil rights and soon submits a civil rights bill to Congress.

JULY 23: Birmingham rescinds the Segregation Ordinances.

SUMMER: Arnetta desegregates restaurants and movie theaters, and Wash eats ice cream at a lunch counter. Students around the country hold protests.

AUGUST 28: James attends March on Washington.

SEPTEMBER 15: Sixteenth Street Baptist Church is bombed, killing four girls, and two boys are shot. Two days later, James carries Carole Robertson's casket.

1964

JULY 2: President Johnson signs the Civil Rights Act of 1964.

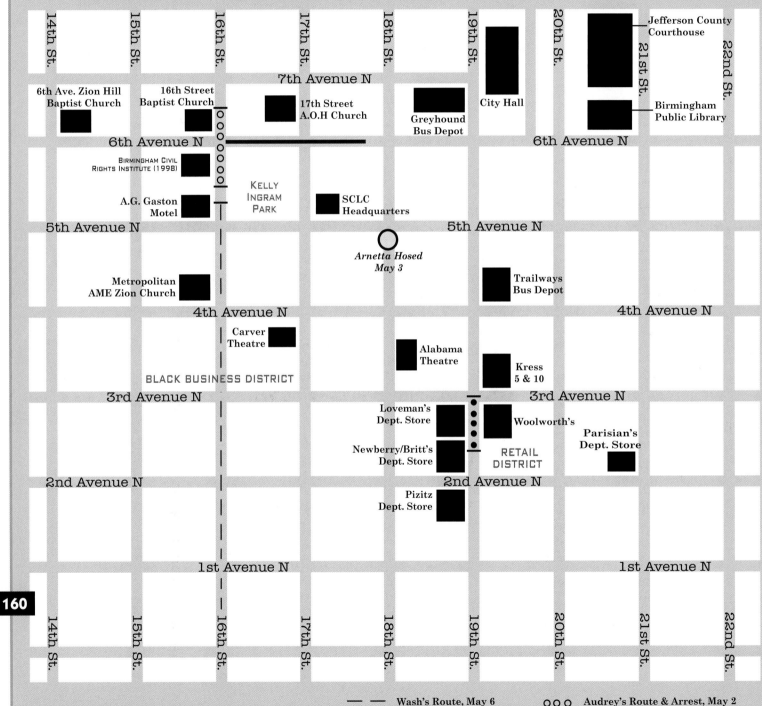

DOWNTOWN DISTRICT

BIRMINGHAM, ALABAMA, 1950s–1960s

14th St.
15th St.
16th St.
17th St.
18th St.
19th St.
20th St.
21st St.
22nd St.

7th Avenue N

6th Ave. Zion Hill Baptist Church

16th Street Baptist Church

17th Street A.O.H Church

Greyhound Bus Depot

City Hall

Jefferson County Courthouse

Birmingham Public Library

6th Avenue N

6th Avenue N

BIRMINGHAM CIVIL RIGHTS INSTITUTE (1998)

A.G. Gaston Motel

KELLY INGRAM PARK

SCLC Headquarters

5th Avenue N

5th Avenue N

Arnetta Hosed May 3

Trailways Bus Depot

Metropolitan AME Zion Church

4th Avenue N

4th Avenue N

Carver Theatre

Alabama Theatre

Kress 5 & 10

BLACK BUSINESS DISTRICT

3rd Avenue N

3rd Avenue N

Loveman's Dept. Store

Woolworth's

Parisian's Dept. Store

Newberry/Britt's Dept. Store

RETAIL DISTRICT

2nd Avenue N

2nd Avenue N

Pizitz Dept. Store

1st Avenue N

1st Avenue N

160

14th St.
15th St.
16th St.
17th St.
18th St.
19th St.
20th St.
21st St.
22nd St.

— — — Wash's Route, May 6   ooo Audrey's Route & Arrest, May 2

●●● Arnetta's First Route, April 20   —— James's Route & Arrest, May 2

THANK YOUs

HOW OFTEN DO YOU GET to meet your heroes? And not just meet them but sit down and talk with them?

Audrey Faye Hendricks, Washington Booker III, Arnetta Streeter Gary, and James W. Stewart are my heroes not only because of what they did when they were young but also because they want you to know their stories. Without the remarkably generous amounts of time, spirit, and candor they shared with me, this book would not exist. I am honored that they trusted me; I fervently hope they feel I have done them justice.

Others I talked with at length— Ricky Shuttlesworth Bester, Richard Boone, Charles Entrekin, Peter and Marian Wright Edelman, Ben and Ellen Cooper Erdreich, Jan Hendricks Fuller, Cleopatra Goree, Stephen Grafman, Randy Kennedy, Bernard Lafayette, Henry Lapedus, Robert and Faye Levin, Andrew Marrisett, Carolyn Maull McKinstry, Chris McNair, Diane McWhorter, Hobart McWhorter, Earl Melton Jr., Pam Walbert Montanaro, Diane Nash, Robert Posey, Rickey Powell, Richard Rabinowitz, Bill Ricker, James Roberson, Dale Russakoff, Susan Levin Schlechter, Tish Oden Spaulding, Lamar Weaver, Gwendolyn Cook Webb, Tara White, Ruth Woods Williams, Abraham Lincoln Woods, Odessa Woolfolk, Tommy Wrenn, among many—deepened the stories.

Heroes come in many forms. Sometimes, they're people who do their jobs exceedingly well. I am especially grateful to two archivists—Laura Anderson at the Birmingham Civil Rights Institute and Jim Baggett at the Birmingham Public Library. I cringe at the possibility that, despite their heroic efforts, errors might remain. Many thanks, too, to my agent-mates and critique partners in Austin— Lynn Brooks, Carole Buckman, Jean LeVitt, Mary Reilly, Polly Robertus—and in Boston—Hillary DeBaun, Joe Lawlor, Patrice Sherman—as well as to Jane Ann Baggett, a most astute young reader.

I wish for everyone the great fortune of having a sister like mine, Judy Brachman, and friends like Joan Bailin, Dinah Chenven, Dena Granof, Frances Hamermesh, Joan Hilgers, Frances Schenkkan, Dale Sonnenberg, and Roberta Wright, who literally cheered me through this process. To my family I am enduringly grateful; I wish blessings on them, just as their lives have blessed mine. Each is an activist or activist-to-be of whom I am profoundly proud.

Finally, I extend deep gratitude to Chris Barton, who referred me to Erin Murphy, who signed me on faith and led me to Kathy Landwehr, who taught me how to transform a manuscript into a book.

ABBREVIATIONS USED
IN SOURCE NOTES

AH: Audrey Hendricks, personal interview

AH/BCRI: Audrey Hendricks, BCRI oral history transcript

ASG: Arnetta Streeter Gary, personal interview

ASG/BCRI: Arnetta Streeter Gary, BCRI oral history transcript

AW: Abraham Woods, personal interview

BL: Bernard Lafayette, personal interview

BN: *Birmingham News*

Branch: Taylor Branch, *Parting the Waters*

BW: *Birmingham World*

CE: Charles Entrekin, personal interview

CM: Carolyn McKinstrey, personal interview

CM/BCRI: Carolyn McKinstrey, BCRI oral history transcript

CP: Connor Papers, Main Branch, Birmingham Public Library. (Note: "Connor Papers" refers to the Birmingham Police Department Inter-Office Communication memoranda prepared by police officers who attended mass meetings.)

DM: Diane McWhorter, personal interview

EF/BCRI: Elizabeth Fitts, BCRI oral history transcript

Eskew: Glenn Eskew, *But for Birmingham*

EW/BCRI: Eileen Walbert, BCRI oral history transcript

Eyes: *Eyes on the Prize*

Force: *A Force More Powerful*

GCW: Gwen Cook Webb, personal interview

GSG/BCRI: Gwendolyn Sanders Gamble, BCRI oral history transcript

Harris: W. Edward Harris, *Miracle in Birmingham*

Hampton: Henry Hampton and Steve Fayer, *Voices of Freedom*

Holt: Len Holt, *Eyewitness*

Huntley: Horace Huntley, *Foot Soldiers for Democracy*

JHF: Jan Hendricks Fuller, personal interview

JS: James Stewart, personal interview

JS/BCRI: James Stewart, BCRI oral history transcript

Kasher: Steven Kasher, *The Civil Rights Movement*

King: Martin Luther King Jr., *Why We Can't Wait*

Lest: "Lest We Forget, I'm On My Way, Volume 2"

Levine: Ellen Levine, *Freedom's Young Children*

LH/BCRI: Lola Hendricks, BCRI oral history transcript

Manis: Andrew Manis, *A Fire You Can't Put Out*

McWhorter: Diane McWhorter, *Carry Me Home*

Mighty: *Mighty Times: The Children's March*

MLK: Martin Luther King Jr.

Nunnelley: William A. Nunnelley, *Bull Connor.*

NYT: *New York Times*

Pacifica: Pacifica Radio Archive

PWM: Pam Walbert Montanaro, personal interview

RBPC: Ruth Barefield-Pendleton Collection (refers to papers available in the box with this name at the BCRI.)

SLS: Susan Levin Schlechter, personal interview

Stanton: Mary Stanton, *Freedom Walk*

Sznajderman: Michael Sznajderman, *A Dangerous Business*

Thornton: J. Mills Thornton, *Dividing Lines*

Ulrich: Joyce Ulrich, *We Were the Heart of the Struggle*

Vaught: Seneca Vaught, *Narrow Cells and Lost Keys*

WB: Washington Booker, personal interview

WB/BCRI: Washington Booker, BCRI oral history transcript

West: Carroll Van West, *The Civil Rights Movement in Birmingham, Alabama, 1933–1979*

White: Marjorie White, *Walk to Freedom*

"BCRI" refers to the Birmingham Civil Rights Institute. Citations notated "BCRI" refer to interviews conducted under the auspices of and available through the Institute.

NOTES

55 "ignoring the...the fight": Eskew, p. 229

55 "the Klan...are not": White, p. 2

55 *the campaign...temporarily abandoned*: "10 More Negroes Seized in Birmingham Sit-Ins"; NYT, 4/6/63

55 "We are...in Birmingham": Eskew p. 230

55 "Can't the...to jail": Thomas T. Coley in the *Birmingham Post-Herald*, April 18, 1963. *www.pbs.rg/wgbh/amex/eyesontheprize/story/07_c.html*

55 "We recognize...and untimely": Thornton, p. 303

56 "Perhaps the...be reconsidered": Robert F. Kennedy in Eyes

56 "We're tired...it now": "The Birmingham Story: Segregation is Teetering Under Fire"; NYT, 5/26/63

56 "There isn't...Mr. Boutwell": Thornton, p. 286

56 "monstrous legislation": McWhorter, p. 313

56 "to stir inter-racial discord": Eskew, p. 222

56 "We will...to Birmingham", Thornton, p. 305

56 "Boutwell's not...'bout well": Woods 5/11/08

56 *I have...man's freedom*: MLK, "Letter from Birmingham Jail"

56 "'Wait' has...meant 'Never'": Eyes

56 "The time...do right": CP, 4/5/63, p. 4

57 *from engaging...the peace*: Eskew, p. 237

57 *Good Friday...is lost*: King, p. 59

58 "if the...Constitutional Mandate": "Ledger: Strategy Committee of The Alabama Christian Movement for Human Rights and Southern Christian Leadership Conference"; RBPC

58 "Stop them": Eskew, pp. 241–42

59 "chicken-eating...Baptist preacher": "James L. Bevel, 72, An Advisor To King"; NYT, 12/23/2008

59 "He had...than us": JS/BCRI, p. 7

59 "Birmingham is sick...stop us": Eskew, p. 242

59 "The Negro...and walked": Branch, p. 735

59 "became the...young people": JS, 1/28/09

59 "Some of...segregated school": Eskew, p. 242

Chapter Seven / The Foot Soldiers
PAGE

61 "[Y]ou are...with him": Hampton, pp. 131–132

62 "A boy...the job": Hampton, p. 131

62 *boy in high school*: Hampton, p. 132

63 "The next...first time": ASG/BCRI, p. 10

63 "I lied...to jail": ASG, 10/24/09

63 "We were...in here?": ASG, 10/31/09

63 "I want my freedom": ASG/BCRI, p. 11

63 "She thought...smart-mouthed": ASG, 10/31/09

63 "in a...to sit": ASG, 10/24/09

63 "The food...extra duties": ASG/BCRI, p. 12

63 "We sang...calmed down": ASG, 6/11/10

63 "I had...looked back": ASG/BCRI, p. 13

64 "What am...the demonstration?": ASG, 10/31/09

64 "You tell...being hardheaded": ASG, 10/31/09

64 "You've done...this alone": ASG, 10/31/09

65 "They were...of us": ASG, 6/11/10

65 "Keep on...on picketing": Stanton, p. 99

66 *End Segregation in America*: Branch, p. 748

66 "run out...could go": Eskew, p. 261

66 "As a responsible...school hours": Manis, p. 368

66 "Sometimes you...them enslaved": Manis, p. 366

68 "You are...to march": Manis, p. 366

68 *to walk...the law*: "Petition for Permit"; RBPC

68 "lot of ...do something": Gwen Cook Webb in Mighty

68 "How I...my business": James Bevel in Mighty

68 "We got...we got": McWhorter, p. 363

69 "It will...we want": Eskew, p. 263

69 "We are...to march": Eskew, p. 263

69 "Nobody stood...us kids": Gwendolyn Sanders Gamble in Mighty

69 *the utter...a dungeon*: King, p. 61

69 "It was...let go": ASG, 6/11/10

69 "just got...said, 'OK'": AH, 1/12/08

69 "When we...of this": CM, 1/10/08

69 "It was...started rolling": CM, 1/10/08

Chapter Eight / May 2. D-Day
PAGE

71 "Good goobly woobly!": McWhorter, p. 360

71 "Timberrrr, let it fall!": McWhorter, p. 360

71 "Kids, there's...be served": Mighty

72 "We never...the destination": GSG/BCRI, p. 14

72 "It's here...the movement": ASG/BCRI, p. 15

72 "running around...cut off": ASG/BCRI, p. 15

72 "A number...in jeopardy": ASG/BCRI, p. 15

72 "And sitting...a stand": Odessa Woolfolk, personal interview, 1/10/08

73 "I had...my left": Andrew Marrisett, personal interview, 5/10/08

98 "It's like…to you": PWM

98 "nigger-knocking in nigger-town": McWhorter 12/3/09

99 "I don't…against integration": Mighty

99 "I was…we didn't": SLS

99 "There's trouble…go": SLS

99 "In Alabama…get out": WB/BCRI, p. 18

99 "They weren't…reading them": CE, 6/16/10

100 "The editors…go away": BN 2/26/06

100 "The teacher…into it": PWM

100 "I was…it changing": PWM

100 "I told…from heaven": PWM

101 "It was…Holy Spirit": PWM

Chapter Eleven / May 4-6, 1963
PAGE

103 "He had…for me!": JS, 10/20/09

103 "[N]obody else…a group": JS/BCRI, p. 13

104 "He would…join in": JS/BCRI, p. 13

104 "when you're…hearts out!": Mighty, Teacher's Guide, p. 15

104 "strolling Negroes": Branch, p. 765

105 "Get off…the movement": Hampton, p. 134

105 "I'm with…like, wow": Eskew, p. 272

107 "there were…Martin King": Burke Marshall in Manis, p. 374

107 "I didn't…basically there": AH/BCRI, p. 10 and AH, 1/12/08

108 "We had…would sleep": JS/BCRI p.11

108 "the toilet…four hundred people": JS/BCRI, p. 11

108 "turned the…the day": JS, 10/20/09

108 "I was at my wits' end": JS, 1/28/09

108 "They…wanted…were Okay": JS/BCRI, p. 13

108 "No blacks…in Birmingham": "Sing for Freedom," Smithsonian Folkways, 1992

109 "We're tired…just walk": Branch, p. 766

109 "You have…we can": Manis, p. 374

109 "Turn on…we die": McWhorter, p. 387

109 "Turn on…the hoses": McWhorter, p. 387

109 "You turn…do that": West, p. 46

109 "We're here…not people": McWhorter, p. 387

109 "the parting of the Red Sea": Manis, p. 375

109 *thirty seconds…Birmingham story*: King, p. 90

110 "The judge…get me": JS, 1/28/09 and 10/20/09

110 "Don't you…down there": WB, 5/12/08

110 "When she…toward downtown": WB, 5/12/08

110 *Fight for…our country*: "Birmingham Jails 1,000 More Negroes"; NYT, 5/7/63

111 "I knew…to jail": WB, 6/12/10

111 "When we…was on!": WB, 5/2/08

111 "Gotta go…gotta go": Huntley, p. xxx

111 "The whole…watching you": McWhorter, p. 392

111 "I should…at home": WB, 6/12/10

111 "Do you…under arrest": Holt, p. 796

112 "I didn't…of liberation": WB, 5/12/08

112 "First they…nappy-headed children": WB/BCRI, p. 15

113 "maybe five hundred…to us": WB, 5/12/08

113 "We started…sang it": WB, 5/12/08

113 "Some of…for us": WB, 5/12/08

113 "As the…rooms filled": AH, 1/12/08

113 "We would…filling up": AH, 1/12/08

113 "It was…wall us": Vaught, p. 145

114 "They were…and released": ASG, 10/24/09

114 "If you…movies downtown": Coffey, p. 802

114 "We all…steel coffin": Miriam McClendon, BCRI oral history transcript

114 "The girls…this way": Mary Hamilton in Pacifica

115 "This is…of mankind": "Martin Luther King Jr. Speaking" on Lest

Chapter Twelve / May 7-10, 1963
PAGE

117 "[T]hose over…from school": BN 5/8/63a

117 "mark[ed] the…a dream": "Negroes Routed At Birmingham"; NYT, 5/8/63

118 "They were…about it": JS, 6/10/10

118 "It was…your budget": WB, 5/12/08

118 "Once you…of you" Dick Gregory in Mighty

118 "Bull Connor…will be": Manis, p. 377

119 *Negroes on…black faces*: King, pp. 93–94

119 "When they…I bathed": Andrew Marrissett, personal interview

120 "What does…of things?": Eskew, p. 282

120 "We want…want to": CP, 5/9/63, p. 6

120 "After dinner…Emancipation Proclamation": CP, 5/9/63, p. 5

120 *outside agitators*: McWhorter, p. 406

120 "If we're…of living": Eskew, p. 279

121 "We're not calling anything off": McWhorter, p. 414

121 "People have…their trouble": Manis, p. 382

122 "with what…the streets": Manis, p. 383

Chapter Thirteen / May 11–May 23

Chapter Fourteen / Freedom and Fury

141   "The first...on it": ASG, 2/9/10

141   "The waitresses...quiet amazement": Eskew, p. 317

141   "I went...the wall": WB, 5/12/08

142   "you could...the window": AH, 1/12/08

142   "We were...weird feeling": JS, 2/10/10

142   "It gave...the system": EW/BCRI, p. 17

142   "Birmingham put...the country" JS, 1/28/09

143   "When a...over America": Eyes

143   "It ought...ignore them": Radio and Television Report to the American People on Civil Rights, June 11, 1963, *http://www.jfklibrary.org/Research/Ready-Reference/JFK-Speeches/Radio-and-Television-Report-to-the-American-People-on-Civil-Rights-June-11-1963.aspx*

144   "people all...were throngs": JS, 2/10/10

145   "the greatest...our nation": MLK, "I Have a Dream"

145   "We knew...national stage": JS, 2/10/10

145   *No student...Birmingham, Alabama*: "Executive Order Number Ten of the Governor of Alabama": September 9, 1963

146   "It was...and gloomy": ASG, 2/9/10

146   "Two minutes": McKinstrey BCRI, p. 17

147   "We should...these men": McWhorter, p. 525

147   "Anything we...of rocks": WB, 6/12/10

147   "All we...get even": WB, 6/23/09

148   "Two of...close friends": JS/BCRI

148   "I stepped...just horrible": JS, 1/28/09

148   "heroines of a holy crusade": White, p. 74

148   "There was...dry eye": ASG, 2/9/10

148   "To know...more determined": JS/BCRI, July 15, 1999, p. 21 and JS, 10/20/09

148   "The death...that bomb": BN, 1/15/09

149   "We are...and bigotry": McWhorter, p. 535

Chapter Fifteen / Afterworld

PAGE
151   "The young...'somebody-ness'": AW, 5/11/08

151   "For the...fought for": AH, 1/12/08 and AH/BCRI, p. 2

152   "warned the...be fired": LH/BCRI, p. 3

152   "an advocate...of purpose": JHF

152   "came back militant": WB/BCRI, p. 19

152   "America had...black people": WB, 4/12/10

153   "We would...defend himself'": WB/BCRI, pp. 20–21

153   "I started...home since": WB, 4/12/10

153   "It's just...been there": WB/BCRI, p. 16

154   "I wanted...possibly could": JS/BCRI, p. 16

154   "I was...all substandard": JS, 12/16/10

155   "I wanted...own children": ASG/BCRI, p. 21

155   "I feel...gives you": ASG, 6/11/10

155   "We had...a change": ASG, 4/28/10

156   "I see...in that'" AH/BCRI, p. 16

156   "the movement...do something" WB/BCRI, pp. 16–17

156   "don't realize...of it": ASG/BCRI, p. 22

156   "abuse all...lives for": GSG/BCRI, p. 16

156   "When my...my heart" AH, 1/12/08

156   "stood on...civil rights": JS, 1/28/09

156   "We've come...the bus": GCW

156   "With commitment, things can change": AH, 1/12/08

156   "are not...were children": JS, 12/15/08

BIBLIOGRAPHY

MANY FINE NONFICTION books, movies, and other sources for young people focus on or include information about Birmingham, Alabama, during the Civil Rights Era. I recommend the following.

Books

Brimner, Larry Dane. *Birmingham Sunday*. Honesdale, Pennsylvania: Boyds Mills Press, 2010.

Levine, Ellen. *Freedom's Children: Young Civil Rights Activists Tell Their Own Stories*. New York: Puffin Books, 1993.

Mayer, Robert H. *When the Children Marched: The Birmingham Civil Rights Movement*. Berkeley Heights, New Jersey: Enslow Publishers, Inc. 2008.

McWhorter, Diane. *A Dream of Freedom: The Civil Rights Movement from 1954 to 1968*. New York: Scholastic, Inc., 2004.

Rochelle, Belinda. *Witnesses to Freedom: Young People Who Fought for Civil Rights*. New York: Dutton Books, 1993.

Tougas, Shelley. Birmingham 1963: *How a Photograph Rallied Civil Rights Support*. Mankato, Minnesota: Compass Point Books, 2011.

Films

Lee, Spike (Director). *4 Little Girls: The story of four young girls who paid the price for a nation's ignorance*. HBO Documentary, 2001. DVD.

Eyes on the Prize: No Easy Walk (1961–1963). Blackside Productions, PBS-TV, 1986. DVD

Mighty Times: The Children's March. Dir. Robert Houston. HBO Family and Southern Poverty Law Center, 2004. DVD

Music

Carawan, Guy and Candie (eds). *Sing for Freedom: The Story of the Civil Rights Movement Through Its Songs*. Montgomery, Alabama: NewSouth Books, 2007.

Seeger, Pete, and Bob Reiser. *Everybody Says Freedom: A History of the Civil Rights Movement in Songs and Pictures*. New York: Norton, 1989.

Various Artists. *Sing for Freedom: The Story of the Civil Rights Movement Through Its Songs*. Smithsonian Folkways, 1992.

Selected Websites

Birmingham Civil Rights Institute
www.bcri.org

Eyes on the Prize
www.pbs.org/wgbh/amex/eyesontheprize/about/fd.html

National Civil Rights Museum
www.civilrightsmuseum.org

The Martin Luther King, Jr. Research and Education Institute
mlk-kpp01.stanford.edu

IN ADDITION TO INTERVIEWS, newspapers, and other primary sources, I relied most heavily on the following books.

Branch, Taylor. *Parting the Waters: America in the King Years, 1954–1963*. New York: Simon and Schuster, 1988.

Eskew, Glenn T. *But for Birmingham: The Local and National Movements in the Civil Rights Struggle*. The University of North Carolina Press, 1997.

McWhorter, Diane. *Carry Me Home: Birmingham, Alabama: The Climactic Battle of the Civil Rights Revolution*. New York: Simon & Schuster, 2001.

Thornton, J. Mills III. *Dividing Lines: Municipal Politics and the Struggle for Civil Rights in Montgomery, Birmingham, and Selma*. Tuscaloosa: The University of Alabama Press, 2006.

PHOTO CREDITS

EVERY EFFORT has been made to trace the ownership of any copyrighted material in this book and to secure permission from holders of the copyright. The publisher would be happy to insert the appropriate acknowledgment in future editions of this book.

Associated Press
12–13, 60–61

Birmingham, Ala. Public Library Archives
4–5 (Martin Luther King Jr., File #1102.2.51.60); 10 (Fred Shuttlesworth, File #829.1.62); 11 (Selective Buying Campaign File #1102.2.3); 15 (Bull Connor, File #827.1.14); 18 (riot in Trailways Bus Station, 827.2.57); 20–21 (lunch counter sit–in, File #827.1.78); 43 (Sidney Smyer, Portrait Collection [Smyer]); 54 (A. D. Porter and A. D. King, File #827.1.70); 58 (Fred Shuttlesworth, Ralph Abernathy, Martin Luther King Jr., File #1125.11.20); 92 (white protesters, File #827.2.21); 94 (postcard, File #1125.7.1), 105 (James Bevel with police, File #1125.11.5b); 146 (Sixteenth Street Baptist church bombing exterior damage, File #85.1.18); 147 (Sixteenth Street Baptist church bombing window damage, File #85.1.17)

Birmingham Civil Rights Institute
67

Birmingham News
17, 46–47, 62, 70–71, 76–77, 80–81, 83, 85, 102–103, 116–117, 138–139

Washington Booker III
13, 152

Jan Hendricks Fuller
5 (inset), 151

Cynthia Levinson
153, 154, 155

Library of Congress
8 (LOT 13088, no. 94), 36–37 (LOT 13088, no. 17), 40 (LC–DIG–highsm–05091 DLC), 90–91 (LC–F81– 43556), 125 (LC–USZ62–128478), 131 (DIG–ppmsca– 04293), 144 (LC–U9– 10363–5), 150–151 (LC–DIG– ppmsca–04298)

Magnum Photo
cover (Bob Adelman, photographer); i (Bob Adelman, photographer); 28–29 (Eve Arnold, photographer); 78 (Bob Adelman, photographer); 112 (Bob Adelman, photographer); 128–129 (Danny Lyon, photographer)

James Stewart
21 (inset), 154

Arnetta Streeter Gary
29, 31, 155

Odessa Woolfolk
26

INDEX